MONETARY POLICIES OF THE UNITED STATES, 1932–1938

MONETARY POLICIES
OF THE
UNITED STATES
1932 - 1938

BY

JAMES DANIEL PARIS

WITH A FOREWORD BY

BENJAMIN HAGGOTT BECKHART

ASSOCIATE PROFESSOR OF BANKING
COLUMBIA UNIVERSITY

NEW YORK : MORNINGSIDE HEIGHTS

COLUMBIA UNIVERSITY PRESS

1938

COPYRIGHT 1938

COLUMBIA UNIVERSITY PRESS, NEW YORK

Foreign agents: OXFORD UNIVERSITY PRESS, *Humphrey Milford, Amen House, London, E.C. 4, England,* AND *B. I. Building, Nicol Road, Bombay, India;* KWANG HSUEH PUBLISHING HOUSE, *140 Peking Road, Shanghai, China;* MARUZEN COMPANY, LTD., *6 Nihonbashi, Tori-Nichome, Tokyo, Japan*

To

M. M. P. *and* R. J. P.

FOREWORD

NOT since the original monetary statutes of 1792 have such far-reaching measures been enacted with respect to the currency as during the first administration of Franklin D. Roosevelt. Never before have such all-extensive powers been conferred on the Executive. The new power to issue greenbacks greatly exceeds that voted by Congress during the Civil War. The President was given the authority to establish bimetallism at any ratio he might find necessary and to reduce by as much as 50 percent the weight of the gold dollar, which, excepting for minor changes in 1834 and 1837, had not been altered since the establishment of the Republic. By a stroke of the pen the gold clause in contracts was abrogated and all forms of currency were given the legal-tender power. The Silver Purchase Act of 1934 made the earlier enactments, the Bland-Allison Act and the Sherman Silver Purchase Act, seem like feeble gestures. The monetary legislation adopted was enacted with little discussion and with little recognition, on the part of the executive and legislative branches of the government, of its significance or implications. Fundamental monetary changes were effected in a nonchalant fashion which ill suited the importance of the occasion.

In so far as they rested on any theoretical basis, the monetary enactments and policies were based on the acceptance of a rigid quantitative theory of money and credit. A mechanical arithmetic relationship was assumed between the price of gold, the quantity of currency and bank deposits on the one hand, and prices and business activity on the other. Through the adoption of suitable monetary measures, it was assumed that commodity prices could be raised and then stabilized on this higher level. No heed was given the contention that the distortions engendered in the price system by the price-raising activities would cause prices to fall and the economic house of cards to collapse if stabilization were attempted. The proponents of the measures and policies adopted maintained that the volume and price of exports bore a direct relationship to increases in the price of gold and silver. It was further assumed that the low rates of interest, resulting from the monetary policies followed, would stimulate the capital markets and that business activity would parallel the growth in the volume of demand deposits accompanying deficit financing.

Recent economic changes give little support to the contentions of the expansionist school of monetary and credit theory. Commodity prices had not attained their 1926 level and business activity had not returned to "normal" before the country was engulfed in the depression of 1937–1938. As heritages of the policies followed are the huge increase in the public debt, which introduces still another element of inflexibility in the economic system, and the large expansion in the capital assets of the commercial banks, which renders them all the more vulnerable to interest rate increases.

Doubtless the precise effects of the policies followed on prices and business activity will always be subject to dispute. In economic change the effect of one course of action cannot be separated from all others. In detailing the monetary enactments and policies followed through this five-year period and in providing data heretofore not generally available, Dr. Paris's study will prove indispensable in the evaluation of results. In presenting the reasons for the policies followed and the consequences flowing therefrom, he has performed signal service. Dr. Paris has added greatly to our understanding of developments during these years, and has furnished a *vade mecum* to all monetary students.

BENJAMIN HAGGOTT BECKHART

COLUMBIA UNIVERSITY
April, 1938

AUTHOR'S PREFACE

THE money and currency measures of the United States Government during the six-year period from early 1932 to early 1938 reflected a succession of changing monetary policies, rather than a single definite, integrated policy. Thus, steps were taken, and not always consciously or consistently, to conserve gold, to increase its monetary value, to permit gold to leave the country, to prohibit it from leaving the country, and to encourage its importation. Some actions were undertaken to stimulate "easy" money, at the same time that others were being taken to prevent a runaway inflation as, for example, the offsetting of gold imports, first by raising reserve requirements, and later by "sterilizing" gold in an "inactive" account of the Treasury.

The silver policies also varied greatly. The Administration at first was willing to tolerate a small increase in the monetary silver stocks through the acceptance of foreign war-debt payments. Then our Government indicated its willingness to "stabilize" the price of silver, as evidenced by the London Conference Treaties. This willingness took concrete form in the Government's subsequent announcement that it would purchase all the newly mined domestic silver. The seeming climax, the step to "nationalize" domestic silver, was capped by the Government's apparent attempt to purchase the whole world's stock of silver, whether needed by other nations for monetary purposes or needed domestically for industrial or other direct consumption purposes. The setting of different prices for each class of silver to be acquired resulted in creating three commodities out of a single, standard commodity. After prosecuting the silver policy vigorously for a year and a half, the Treasury lost some of its erstwhile eagerness, and toward the end of 1937 was purchasing only 20 million ounces of silver per month as compared with almost 100 million ounces in some of the latter months of 1935.

The national bank-note issue was given an enormous fillip

in July, 1932, but before three years elapsed these bank notes had been deprived of even the privilege to exist. Not only did the extended privileges granted in 1932 expire, but those which had existed before 1932 were withdrawn—privileges, it is true, which had been continued since 1930 only at the sufferance of the Secretary of the Treasury and indirectly, of course, of the Administration.

In only one regard can the series of policies be considered as consistent. That is in their tendency towards the concentration and centralization of monetary powers in the hands of the Federal Government. Despite pleas that each of the measures was undertaken as an emergency measure, one emergency after another seemed to crop up. The subsequent extension of the time limit for all of the "emergency" monetary and currency laws suggests that these laws will eventually become a permanent part of our legislation. For after the economic system has become accustomed to operate in their climate, as it were, it may be almost impossible to effect any fundamental reversion to the former monetary standard.

It might be argued that these gyrations in policy were forced upon the United States, first by economic and monetary changes abroad, secondly by foreign political uncertainties, and then by the recurring war scares which chased frightened capital to American shores. It cannot be denied, however, that the United States has been at least partially responsible for foreign economic conditions, and perhaps to some extent for the state of political affairs. But in a world in which economics and politics are so inextricably interwoven, it is not easy to point out the culprit for each little increment to the top-heavy burden of economic and political disturbances, many of which are rooted in a war of world-wide and long-lasting consequence.

This book will trace the various recent monetary policies of the United States, starting in early 1932 and coming down through the early part of 1938. It will first describe the conditions antecedent to the steps taken. Then the immediate legislative measures adopted will be analyzed, as will the subsequent orders, rules, regulations, and so forth which stemmed from the laws enacted. There will follow a description of the definitive actions undertaken to carry out the laws, and of the subsequent results. A concluding section will be devoted to an appraisal of the several policies, both as to the objectives sought and as to the results which actually ensued.

In the preparation of this study I am especially indebted to Professor James W. Angell and Professor Benjamin Haggott Beckhart for their considerate reading of the manuscript. Discussion with other members of the Columbia University Faculty, and with members of downtown financial institutions, has helped toward the clarification of disputed points. Thanks are due to Professor Horace Taylor and to Professor Frederick E. Croxton, whose encouragement, however intangible, proved nonetheless a real stimulation. Finally, my wife, Margaret Maher Paris, deserves no small measure of praise, both for her helpful criticisms and for her assumption of the burdensome task of seeing the book through the press. Needless, perhaps, to state, responsibility for the conclusions contained herein are the author's alone.

JAMES D. PARIS

PELHAM, NEW YORK
April, 1938

CONTENTS

CHARTS

MONETARY POLICIES OF THE UNITED STATES, 1932–1938

I

UNDERLYING CONDITIONS, 1931–1933

THE five years beginning in February, 1932, witnessed a series of extensive alterations in the monetary system of the United States which resulted in completely reconstituting the basis of a system that had experienced but slight changes in about a century. True, the redefinition of the fineness of United States coins and the small variation made in the ratio of gold to silver, in 1834 and 1837, did reduce the weight of the gold dollar by 6 percent; and the monetary law of 1873 did virtually establish a single as against a bimetallic standard. But these were more in the nature of legalizing what already obtained *de facto,* or what was urgently demanded by the relationship then current between silver and gold. The innovations begun in 1932, on the other hand, were deliberate manipulations of a going monetary system to further a variety of ends, ends which varied month by month, and almost day by day. First it was thought desirable to protect our gold stock, then our price level, then our monetary system, then the value of our money in foreign exchange, then our foreign trade, depending upon the interests which were dominant from day to day. With the objectives at such cross-purposes, small wonder then that the resulting policies and their execution were inconsistent. Instead of meshing with each other, the policies clashed time and again. This resulted in overnight changes in the angles from which attacks were made, involving the setting-up of international agreements upon a twenty-four-hour basis, the establish-ment of a two-billion-dollar exchange stabilization fund for which the President and the Secretary of the Treasury were to be accountable to no one, and the granting to the President of extraordinary discretionary powers.

THE BANKING CRISIS, FEBRUARY–MARCH, 1933

President Roosevelt was inaugurated on March 4, 1933, in the midst of financial chaos. Banks had been forced to close their doors because of the devastating spread of bank runs. What had started as a comparatively small run upon banks in one state, Michigan, resulting in the proclaiming of an eight-day banking holiday there on February 14, gathered speed and momentum, landing first in one part of the country and then in another. That proclamation "proved the opening signal of alarm which rapidly extended from one state to another, until on March 4, practically every bank in the nation was closed."[1]

Indiana followed Michigan by only nine days in declaring a bank holiday. Then came in quick succession, Maryland, Arkansas, and Ohio. On the first day of March, Alabama, Kentucky, Tennessee, and Nevada declared holidays. The next day states as far apart as Oregon and Mississippi declared holidays. On March 3, Georgia, the State of Washington, and five others succumbed. Then on March 4, the crowning stroke occurred as New York, Illinois, and twenty-three other states proclaimed holidays, thus closing the banks in practically the entire nation. By that date most of the banks throughout the country were either closed or were operating under restrictions.

The banking crisis did not spring full-born from events which occurred in the middle of February. Nor were the happenings in 1932 at the root of the trouble, even though that year did see the beginning of proclamations of "bank holidays" and "bank moratoria" on a significant scale. During 1932, many banks in a number of states had closed temporarily under special "banking holidays" declared by civil authorities. In November, a state-wide banking moratorium was declared by the Governor of Nevada. Banks in other states, while not actually ceasing business, obtained agreements from their depositors for the postponement or waiver of their claims. The developments which led to the crisis were even further removed in time.

The banking crisis early in 1933 was a culmination of developments that had been under way since the beginning of the depression in 1929 and in many areas for a considerably longer period. One of the outstanding characteristics of the depression had been the successive outbreaks of acute banking difficulties that began in 1930 and continued to recur from time to time until March 1933. Between the end of December 1929 and the end of February 1933

[1] United States Department of Commerce, *World Economic Review*, 1933, p. 15.

nearly 5,000 banks, or more than one bank in every five, suspended operations, with deposit liabilities aggregating about $3,500,000,000.

The first series of these failures came in the latter part of 1930 in Kentucky, Tennessee, Arkansas, and North Carolina, followed by suspension of a large bank in New York and another in Philadelphia. Conditions improved early in 1931, but there was another and even more widespread series of failures from the middle of 1931 until February 1932. This series started with suspension of a large number of banks in Chicago and the surrounding region and spread to Ohio and other Midwestern States, to Pennsylvania and New York, and toward the end of 1931 to New England.

Following the formation of the Reconstruction Finance Corporation in February 1932 the rate of suspensions was substantially reduced. In June and July 1932, however, banking difficulties again occurred in Chicago and surrounding territory. During the remainder of 1932, until December, there were relatively few failures and most of these were among small banks. In December 1932 suspensions began to increase and in the first 6 weeks of 1933 they became more numerous and more widespread and involved more banks of substantial size. The volume of deposits of suspended banks was particularly large in southern New Jersey, the District of Columbia, Tennessee, Illinois, Iowa, Missouri, Nevada, and California. Finally, renewed banking difficulties in February 1933 led to the temporary closing of all banks by official action, first in the State of Michigan, then in other States, and finally by Presidential proclamation throughout the country.[2]

The immediate conditions preceding the crisis reflected the cumulated effects of the sharp recession in business and industrial activity which had been in process for some three and a half years. Concomitant factors, naturally, were the precipitous declines in commodity, security and real-estate prices. These declines intensified the inability of debtors to meet their obligations. Creditors became panicky and called, or refused to extend, their outstanding loans. By the end of 1932, deflationary forces were in full swing. Bank suspensions were increasing daily and general debt defaults rose acceleratingly. Hoarding, both domestic and foreign, was becoming more evident. Foreigners had been withdrawing their dollar balances since the last few months of 1931, and draining gold from the United States.

[2] Federal Reserve Board, *Annual Report,* 1933, pp. 3, 4.

Signs pointing toward the intensification of domestic hoarding were seen in the following occurrences: in January, 1933, the post-holiday return flow of the currency was less than usual; in February, actual withdrawals of currency took place, in substantial amounts in the aggregate; and during this period the shifting of deposits became widespread. The shifting of deposits was evidenced by the transfer from banks in one part of a community, or of the country, to other parts, and from banks to other institutions. Toward the end of February there developed fears for the future convertibility of the currency, and gold withdrawals, which had been moderate, reached a more acute stage.

The drains upon the domestic banking system engendered a pressure which was felt not only by the weaker small-town banks, but also by the larger city banks and even by the Federal Reserve Banks, which had been paying out Federal Reserve notes and gold.

NATION-WIDE BANKING HOLIDAY

On Monday March 6, 1933, President Roosevelt issued a proclamation declaring a banking holiday for all banking institutions and their branches. The holiday was to be in effect throughout the United States and its possessions, and was to continue through March 9. By the proclamation, all banking transactions were suspended except for those authorized by the Secretary of the Treasury with the approval of the President. Also, the President placed an embargo upon gold exports.

On March 9, the President asked the Congress, which he had convened in extra session, for the immediate enactment of legislation to clarify and augment his authority in a period of national emergency and to promote the reëstablishment of banking facilities. Legislation enacted on the same day granted the President all the powers which he requested. The legislation consisted of the Emergency Banking Act which

(1) confirmed the President's proclamation of March 6, (2) required the Treasury's approval for the reopening of banks, (3) empowered the President to investigate, regulate, or prohibit transactions in gold or foreign exchange, (4) authorized the Comp-

troller of the Currency to appoint conservators for national banks the condition of whose assets did not permit them to open, (5) provided for the purchase by the Reconstruction Finance Corporation of preferred shares in order to facilitate the reorganization of weak banks, (6) authorized the Federal Reserve banks to issue Federal Reserve bank notes secured by United States Government bonds or commercial paper (in the latter case up to 90 percent of the estimated value), and (7) granted the member banks wider access to the Federal Reserve banks for the emergency period.[3]

On March 9, 1933, the holiday was continued by the President until further proclamation, and indeed on December 16, 1936, at the Treasury Department Appropriation Bill Hearings Mr. C. F. Ellis, of the office of the General Counsel of the Treasury Department, stated[4] that the bank holiday was still in effect even at that late date.

The bank-holiday proclamation and the subsequent steps taken thereunder became the opening wedge for the Administration in its endeavor to take over and practically "nationalize" the financial mechanism of the nation. Under the plea of "emergency" and pursuant to emergency powers granted in the Trading-with-the-Enemy Act of 1917, the banking system, the monetary system, and even the capital market were brought under the control of the Federal Government. Additional control through deficit financing and other indirect and unplanned means gave the Government control over interest rates, the disposition of corporate earnings, business operations, and other elements of administration and management. The potentialities embraced in the steps taken, and in the authorizations granted, are all but limitless. If the central government control the money and credit machinery, so vital to the present, capitalistic, business economy as we know it, what is to prevent it from eventually assuming management of the whole economic structure, comprehending thus in its grasp every activity from the output of the raw materials to final consumption by the individual? This is undoubtedly the goal of some of the "economic planners," but the insolvable complications involved have been demonstrated too often even to need comment.

[3] United States Department of Commerce, *World Economic Review*, 1933, p. 15.
[4] Page 81 of the printed *Hearings* before the House Committee on Appropriations.

IMPORTANCE OF MONEY IN THE BUSINESS ECONOMY

It may be argued that monetary considerations are but one group of phenomena in our economy and do not merit the care and attention lavished upon them. But a business economy based upon a price system—that is, an economy predicated not upon the performance of certain acts and services as such, for their own sake, or for any direct benefit derived therefrom, but only in so far as they are productive of a money price—depends for its very existence upon the money and credit structure. We do not produce goods to consume, we produce them to sell, and we must be able to sell them at a price higher than the cost at which they were produced. This heretofore integrated system of prices needs for its efficient functioning a comparatively fixed and stable monetary structure, not one subject to the tug of political whim following whatever will-o'-the-wisp happens to attract at the moment. Abundant resources, technological improvement, transportation facilities, and commodity plenty, all mean nothing if the distributive system, based as it is upon an integrated, interrelated price mechanism, does not function. Unless the business community can have confidence that the price system rests upon a relatively fixed standard rather than upon political convenience or fancy, the capitalistic system, as we know it, is subject to a more or less complete metamorphosis.

I do not mean to imply that a change in the monetary system would immediately produce corresponding changes in the price structure or in price levels. Commodity prices will lag somewhat behind the price of gold, but, unless sufficient offsetting factors develop, they will catch up eventually.

If we stabilize at 59.06 cents of our old gold dollar, calling the value represented by this amount of gold the new dollar, sooner or later commodity prices will rise to a level about 69.3 per cent higher than they would have been had the old gold dollar been retained. This rise in prices, of course, would take time, and the advance would not assume much importance until in some way or other an increased demand for goods and services should be created; for the mere reduction of the gold content of the dollar and the mere pumping of more money and bank credit into circulation will not of themselves raise prices.[5]

This analysis seems nearer the truth than the conclusions reached by the Commission of Inquiry into National Policy in International Economic Relations and summarized by its chairman, Dr. Robert M. Hutchins.

We came to the conclusion in the first place that there is only a minor relationship between the official prices of gold or silver and the general price level. As a matter of fact the official prices of gold and silver have an important influence only on the prices of those commodities which figure largely in international trade. The attempt to raise the domestic price level by raising the price of gold and the price of silver was bound to fail, and it has failed. The attempt was made to promote domestic recovery. It has not succeeded. Indeed the only effect this attempt has had on domestic recovery has been to slow it down. But many people have the delusion that the official price of gold and silver has something to do with the general price level.

In general, monetary policy plays a relatively minor rôle in either domestic or international recovery. Moving the official price of gold or silver up or down does not seem to be the most effective means toward either.[6]

ECONOMIC CONTROL MEASURES, ESPECIALLY MONETARY, TAKEN BY THE UNITED STATES GOVERNMENT, 1932-1937

It was not only through monetary and financial measures that the Administration tried to control the economy of the country. It resorted also to direct means, as, for example, through the National Recovery Administration and the Agricultural Adjustment Administration. But both of these types of regulation, as administered under their respective Acts, were considered unconstitutional by the United States Supreme Court.

The more comprehensive control, but not the less effective because of its hidden and subtle nature, was upheld by the Supreme Court when that Court validated the laws abrogating the gold clause. The circumstances leading up to the enactment of that law and the consequences thereof will be considered in

[5] E. W. Kemmerer, *Kemmerer on Money*, pp. 206, 207.
[6] *Economic Forum* (summer, 1935), pp. 146, 147.

the next chapter, which contains also a discussion of the devaluation of the gold dollar, of gold "sterilization," and so forth.

The subsidies granted to an industry which is of small importance in the economy of the nation as a whole (although large in some of the states), under the guise of monetary and price recovery measures, brings the silver problem to the fore as another aspect of the monetary policies of the Roosevelt Administration. The tremendous pressure exerted by a small but powerful group, starting from a small industrial springboard and landing in the pool of international money and finance, with a resulting world-wide monetary upheaval, drew from the Administration one of the most amazing series of promises and performances ever witnessed. The manipulations of this small group of silver advocates, and the concessions they obtained from the Administration in its policy of "doing something for silver," form the third chapter of this book.

Other types of money, such as Federal Reserve notes, Federal Reserve bank notes, and national bank notes are dealt with in later chapters. While any actions taken in regard to these types of currency are not basically as significant as are the measures undertaken in connection with gold and silver policies, they do reflect to some extent the monetary trends of the Government. It is true, too, that the initial steps altering our currency system were taken in 1932, during the Hoover regime. The first breach was the substitution of Federal obligations for gold as backing for Federal Reserve notes.[7] A few months later the next step was taken by extending the list of bonds given the privilege of serving as backing for national bank notes. These steps were halting, however, and gave not the slightest hint as to the revolutionary changes then impending.

Another interesting point may be mentioned in passing. The simplification of the United States monetary system, for which economists have made pleas time and again, is in a fair way to being effected, but seemingly in a way far different from what they had contemplated. A monetary system whose paper money, outside the Treasury and Central Bank, consists of only Federal Reserve notes, and silver certificates is a picture simple

---

[7] But only above the 40 percent minimum gold requirement.

and bare of adornment, when compared with the former interesting if confusing array of gold certificates, silver certificates, United States notes, Treasury notes of 1890, Federal Reserve notes, Federal Reserve bank notes, and national bank notes.

Another small step in the simplification process was the withdrawal of gold coin from circulation, melting it down, and forming it into bars to be held by the Treasury. But simplification of a monetary system by substituting for convertible currency paper which is irredeemable in gold, or redeemable in silver with a market value of less than half the face value indicated on the currency, is probably not the simplification so earnestly sought heretofore.

II

DELIBERATE MANIPULATION OF THE GOLD DOLLAR

WHEN President Hoover, in his opening campaign speech at Des Moines on October 4, 1932, stated that the "Secretary of the Treasury informed me [winter of 1931–32] that unless we could put into effect a remedy, we could not hold to the gold standard but two weeks longer because of inability to meet the demands of foreigners and our own citizens for gold," the Democratic party rose in wrathful indignation. Even Senator Glass, in a telegram to the New York *Times,* sent on October 7 from a sickbed, denied that any spokesman for the administration privately or publicly expressed the "slightest concern over the gold standard," but on the contrary "scouted the idea that there was the remotest chance of anything of the kind." He seemed, too, to indicate that even the thought of such a thing happening was beyond the bounds of all possibility.

LOSS OF GOLD, 1931–1932

Whatever the charges and countercharges, the external drain upon the United States gold stock, during the autumn of 1931 and the spring of 1932, did threaten the monetary base. (See Chart I.) It totaled more than $1,000,000,000—a sizable chunk to tear off the monetary base within the space of less than a year. By the end of June, 1932, the monetary gold stock of the United States had fallen 20 percent from its mid-1931 figure of $5,000,000,000, which, up to that time, was the highest point that our gold stock had ever reached.

This large gold drain was rooted in the suspension of the gold standard by England, on September 21, 1931. When England left gold, other nations also halted the workings of the gold standard, either completely or partially. The subsequent loss of confidence in the holding of balances abroad, and the desire to strengthen their own gold position, led many central banks, other banking institutions and private firms to withdraw gold from the United States. Also, the decline in domestic confidence, resulting from the foreign demands on our gold, led to internal withdrawals of currency for hoarding. The double threat to the reserves of our banking system by the heavy outward flow of gold, and the accelerating domestic demand for currency, led to a period of acute credit contraction during the last quarter of 1931 and the first quarter of 1932.

Chart I

NET CHANGES IN THE MONETARY GOLD STOCK OF THE UNITED STATES

(Net Increase [+] or Net Decrease [—], by Months)

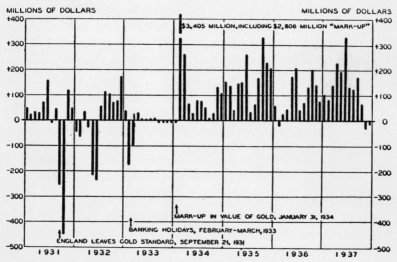

Sources: United States Treasury Department; Board of Governors of the Federal Reserve System.

The export of gold from the United States, in the six weeks following England's suspension of the gold standard, reduced our monetary gold stock by $725,000,000—the largest movement for a similar period in any country at any time. The temporary let-up in the movement, toward the end of the year, was resumed in January and February, and was intensified in May and June, 1932, so that by the end of the nine-months' period since September, 1931, the monetary gold stock had fallen by $1,100,000,000.

The Federal Reserve Board described the situation as follows:

Suspension of the gold standard in England not only tended to immobilize foreign balances still held in London but also to impair confidence in such balances held elsewhere and to cause European banks to convert large portions of their foreign funds into gold. Since a large part of the realizable short-term foreign balances of the world was held in the United States, it was largely upon this country that this movement then concentrated. As a consequence, the United States lost $725,000,000 of gold from the middle of September to the end of October [1931]. About three-fifths of this gold was taken by France, and the bulk of the remainder by Belgium, Switzerland, and Netherlands. These were the countries which previously had been drawing heavily upon the Bank of England's reserves, and which continued to draw gold from the London bullion market when the bank itself ceased to pay out gold. To a considerable extent the movement reflected the desire of the central banks in these countries to increase their metallic reserves with a view to showing a stronger gold position.

In the final two months of 1931 the general movement of the first of the year was resumed, and gold stock in the United States rose as a result of shipments from Canada, Latin America, and the Far East. The flow from these areas had in fact never ceased; but from the middle of September through October, the shipments to Europe had been much larger than the receipts from other parts of the world. In November and December, however, exports to Europe practically ceased, while shipments from Japan, which was endeavoring to maintain the gold standard, were in heavy volume. Even after Japan abandoned the gold standard on December 13, Japanese gold continued to arrive at San Francisco. In these two months the monetary gold stock of the United States increased by $170,000,000.

During 1931 as a whole, the monetary gold stock of the United States decreased by about $135,000,000.[1]

But the year 1932, on the whole, showed a net increase in monetary gold stocks. The violent fluctuations in both the size and the direction of the gold flows in that year are attested to by the decrease in gold stocks of almost half a billion dollars in May and June, as contrasted with an increase of almost $200,000,000 in December. The resulting net increase, for the year as a whole, amounted to $53,000,000.

[1] Federal Reserve Board, *Annual Report,* 1931, p. 11.

During the first half of 1932, the external loss of gold and the internal loss of currency were the predominant factors. Thus the continued pressure upon the banking system called forth Federal Reserve purchase of Governments. These were of large enough volume to enable banks not only to satisfy both the external and internal demands but also to reduce their indebtedness to the Federal Reserve Banks. In the second half of 1932 (beginning about the middle of July), the direction of the gold movement and that of currency were reversed. The monetary gold stock increased by more than $50,000,000 in July, by more than $100,000,000 in the next two months, and by around $75,000,000, in October and November. Also, the banking system was enabled to increase its reserves from two other sources, namely, the return flow of currency, and issue of new national bank notes.

The external and internal drains of gold and currency, as described in Chapter I, were part of the immediate cause of the banking crisis early in 1933. Also of large, but non-measurable, importance was the publication, in December, 1932, of the list of banks and other institutions which had borrowed from the Reconstruction Finance Corporation. Publication of this list made known to depositors and others the extent to which their own banks had had to resort to the Reconstruction Finance Corporation. The resulting loss of confidence was merely one more unbalancing item piled upon the top of an already trembling structure.

BANK HOLIDAY; GOLD RESTRICTIONS

The panic conditions in the financial machinery of the country which finally developed by March 4, 1933, could lead to but one thing, and that was wholesale cessation of activity by a sick body, until it could be nursed back to health *in toto*. Piecemeal measures, such as had been tried by the National Credit Corporation, by the Reconstruction Finance Corporation, by Federal Reserve policy, and by the Glass-Steagall Amendment to the Federal Reserve Act, could not succeed. The closing of the banks, which was all but nation-wide by March 4, 1933, needed to be made complete before a new start could be made. Only one day after his inauguration, President Roosevelt issued the momentous Bank Holiday Proclamation, to go into effect the next day, and to remain in effect until March 9. The broad powers granted in a national emergency by an old law, the Trading-with-the-Enemy Act of October 6, 1917, permitted the President to assume complete and unequivocal control of the nation's whole banking, financial, and monetary machinery. The proclamation effected suspension of all banking transactions except those permitted by the Secretary of the Treasury, and "prohibited the paying out, exporting or earmarking of gold or silver coin or bullion, or currency, or dealing in foreign exchange during the banking holiday."

The special session of Congress convened by the President on March 9 passed the Emergency Banking Act. This Act approved and confirmed the actions already taken by the President, and amended the Act of October 6, 1917. In addition to purely banking provisions, the Act authorized the Secretary of the Treasury to require the delivery of all gold coin, bullion, and certificates to the Treasurer. Also, pursuant to the powers granted by the Act, the President continued the March 6 proclamation until further notice. That is, the banking holiday was extended, as were the prohibitions on gold exports and the restrictions on the paying out of gold by the banks.

On the next day, March 10, the President issued an executive order "under authority specifically confirmed in the emergency act of March 9," in which he prohibited the export of gold coin, bullion, and certificates except by license from the Secretary of the Treasury, and limited foreign exchange to "legitimate and normal business requirements, for reasonable traveling and other personal requirements, and for the fulfillment of contracts entered into prior to March 6, 1933." The order applied not only to individuals, partnerships, associations, corporations and so forth, but also specified that "permission given to banking institutions to perform banking functions should not include authorization to pay out gold coin, gold, or gold certificates, except as authorized by the Secretary of the Treasury." The Secretary of the Treasury stated that,

"Gold continued to be available, however, for use in industry and the arts."[2]

On April 5, 1933, the President issued still another executive order, "nationalizing" gold by forbidding the hoarding of gold coin, bullion or certificates, and requiring all persons to deliver such to a Federal Reserve Bank or branch or agency except for "reasonable amounts for use in industry and the arts, and rare coins, and a maximum of $100 per person in gold coin and gold certificates." The order permitted the holding and acquisition of gold for industrial use and for proper transactions not involving hoarding. Member banks were required to deliver all gold coin, bullion and certificates owned by them or received by them to the Federal Reserve Banks of their respective districts.

On April 13, it was learned that the Treasury Department had licensed an export of gold to Holland against an exchange transaction. This was the first shipment, except for earmarked stock, which the Government had permitted from the United States since the embargo of March 6.

SUSPENSION OF THE GOLD STANDARD

In spite of this indication of the maintenance of the dollar on a gold basis, it was widely thought that ultimate currency depreciation was inevitable. This belief was strengthened by the growing sentiment in Congress for monetary inflation to include the expansion of the use of silver, and the devaluation of the gold dollar. Less than a week later, on April 18, refusal to grant licenses for shipment of gold abroad was made by the Treasury, and on the next day the Secretary of the Treasury

[2] "On March 13th the Secretary of the Treasury authorized the Federal Reserve Banks to sell gold bullion for legitimate and customary trade uses, in such amounts as the banks deemed reasonable, provided the applicant submitted an affidavit stating the amount of unmanufactured gold on hand, and the fact that the procuring of the desired metal was essential to the maintenance of employment. This arrangement continued in force until April 29th, when the procedure of withdrawal was changed in detail under new regulations issued by the Secretary of the Treasury. These regulations merely required an amplification of information and records through a system of affidavits, and were revised from time to time to secure greater control. However, the Government continued to furnish gold bars to the arts and industries at $20.67 per ounce until August 28th." Handy and Harman, *Annual Review*, 1933, p. 42.

advised that "until further notice no further licenses would be granted for the export of gold from the United States for the purpose of supporting the dollar in foreign exchange." On the twentieth the President finally took the nation off the gold standard by the issuance of an executive order which forbade earmarking for foreign account and embargoed the export of gold coin, bullion, and certificates, with the certain exceptions granted through the Secretary of the Treasury.

On April 29, there was some let-up in the stringent gold regulations. The arts and industry, as well as the dealers supplying them, were permitted to purchase gold from the Federal Reserve Banks. Also, exports of earmarked gold, of gold imported for reëxport, and of gold necessary for the fulfillment of a contract entered into before April 20 were permitted.

The next item of importance in the long, varied, and often contradictory list of gold actions occurred on May 7, when the President gave his Sunday evening "fireside" talk over the radio. He stated that as there was not enough gold to pay all holders of gold obligations, the Government should "in the interest of justice" allow none to be paid in gold.

"THOMAS" INFLATION AMENDMENT

The tremendous inflationary pressure which began to become manifest at about this time resulted in the so-called "Thomas" Amendment to the Agricultural Adjustment Act (Title III of the Act of May 12, 1933) .[3] Under this Amendment, the President was authorized, among other things,

---

[3] Following is a brief summary of this Amendment:
Purposes
    (1) To stabilize domestic prices
    (2) To protect our foreign commerce against foreign currency depreciation
    (3) To expand money and credit
Measures to be taken to achieve these purposes
    (1) Expand Federal Reserve credit by \$3,000,000,000
    (2) Issue fiat currency up to \$3,000,000,000
    (3) Reduce weight of gold dollar by up to 50 percent
    (4) Provide for unlimited coinage of gold and silver
    (5) Accept silver from foreign Governments as payments upon their debt to the United States. Only 400,000,000 ounces, at 50 cents per ounce, is to be accepted, and that within the succeeding six months only

by proclamation to fix the weight of the gold dollar . . . and also to fix the weight of the silver dollar . . . at a definite fixed ratio in relation to the gold dollar at such amounts as he finds necessary from his investigation to stabilize domestic prices or to protect the foreign commerce against the adverse effect of depreciated foreign currencies, and to provide for the unlimited coinage of such gold and silver at the ratio so fixed . . . and . . . the weight of the gold dollar . . . so fixed, shall be the standard unit of value . . . but in no event shall the weight of the gold dollar be fixed so as to reduce its present weight by more than 50 per centum.

SUSPENSION OF THE GOLD CLAUSE

The first phase of the Administration's gold policy culminated in Public Resolution Number 10, more generally known as the Joint Resolution of June 5, 1933, which stated, among other provisions, that "every provision contained in or made with respect to any obligation which purports to give the obligee a right to require payment in gold or a particular kind of coin or currency, or in an amount in money of the United States measured thereby, is declared to be against public policy; and no such provision shall be contained in or made with respect to any obligation hereafter incurred." Not only were future "gold clauses" prohibited, but "gold clauses" already a part of obligations then outstanding also were abrogated. This law likewise made "all coins and currencies of the United States (including Federal Reserve notes and circulating notes of Federal Reserve banks and national banking associations) heretofore or hereafter coined or issued," "legal tender for all debts, public and private."

LONDON ECONOMIC CONFERENCE

The rest of June was spent in preparing for the World Monetary and Economic Conference at London, which it was hoped would settle once and for all the monetary policies of the entire world. The preliminary conversations held by President Roosevelt during April and May with Herriot, MacDonald, Jung, and others had paved the way for a smooth and final disposition of the problems under consideration. Furthermore, the Conference was expected to succeed because, as President

Roosevelt said in his May 7 "fireside" talk, one of the objectives of the Conference was "the setting up of a stabilization of currencies, in order that trade and commerce can make contracts ahead. . . The great international conference that lies before us must succeed. The future of the world demands it and we have each of us pledged ourselves to the best joint efforts to that end."

Instead of opening with hope, however, the Conference opened amid fear and distrust. Conversations previously held and promises tacitly made were forgotten. Also, the absorption of the United States in domestic price-raising schemes made her interest in international problems only secondary. The opening on June 12 was anything but auspicious, especially with MacDonald's unexpected reference to the war debts, a question which it had been understood was not to be brought up. Considering the atmosphere of foreboding in which the Conference started, small wonder then that the breakdown of the Conference began even before the echo of the maiden speech had died out.

The action which all but sounded the death knell for the Conference was the sending of a message to the Conference by President Roosevelt on July 2, 1933. He started the message by saying he "would regard it as a catastrophe amounting to a world tragedy" if the Conference should concern itself with foreign exchange stabilization. He continued his "lecture" to the Conference in detailing the problems it should take up and those which it should leave alone. His preoccupation with domestic problems was illustrated by the paragraph in which he said that "the United States seeks the kind of a dollar which a generation hence will have the same purchasing and debt-paying power as the dollar we hope to attain in the near future."

The debilitating shock which was felt by world confidence, and the sickening reaction upon the economic structure which had faintly perceived a ray of light, cannot be described. While one should not try to belittle the nature of the blow, it should be pointed out that the United States was not alone responsible for the step taken by President Roosevelt. Great Britain, whose words sought stability but whose deeds belied them, was not entirely blameless. True, she did want stability, but only upon terms which left little if any room for compromise.

During the remaining weeks of July and during August, the American people forgot world problems, and became concerned with the success of internal recovery measures undertaken through the National Recovery Administration and the establishment of codes. But by the end of August, it became evident that gold and gold policy were still prominent in the President's mind. On August 28, in an executive order, the President revoked the executive orders of April 5 and April 20, and issued comprehensive provisions with respect to the acquisition, hoarding, export, and earmarking of gold coin, bullion and currency, and with respect to transactions in foreign exchange. The August 28 order also required the delivery to the Federal Reserve Banks of all gold coin, gold bullion, or gold certificates domestically held, with certain stated exceptions. Information on holdings and acquisitions of gold and gold certificates was demanded too.

NEWLY MINED DOMESTIC GOLD

On the next day, August 29, 1933, the President issued an executive order authorizing the Secretary of the Treasury to receive all newly mined gold of domestic origin. The gold was to be accepted on consignment for sale either to persons licensed to acquire gold for use in the domestic arts, industry, and professions, or to foreign purchasers for export.

This newly mined domestic gold was to be received by any mint or assay office at a daily price, in terms of our then depreciated currency, which was to equal the highest price obtaining in any of the free gold markets of the world. This program got under way by September 8. The price at which the Secretary of the Treasury was authorized to sell the gold was set at $29.62 per fine ounce on that date. (See Chart II.) From that date to October 25, when the Reconstruction Finance Corporation took up the task, the price set for gold varied from as low as $29.10, on September 11, to as high as $32.28 on September 20.

MOVEMENT "TOWARD A MANAGED CURRENCY"

For almost two months the situation with respect to gold remained quiescent. But on October 22, 1933, the President delivered a radio speech in the course of which he stated that the definite policy of the Government "has been to restore commodity price levels," and after the price level has been re-

Chart II

GOLD PURCHASE PRICES OF THE UNITED STATES GOVERNMENT
(In Dollars per Fine Ounce)

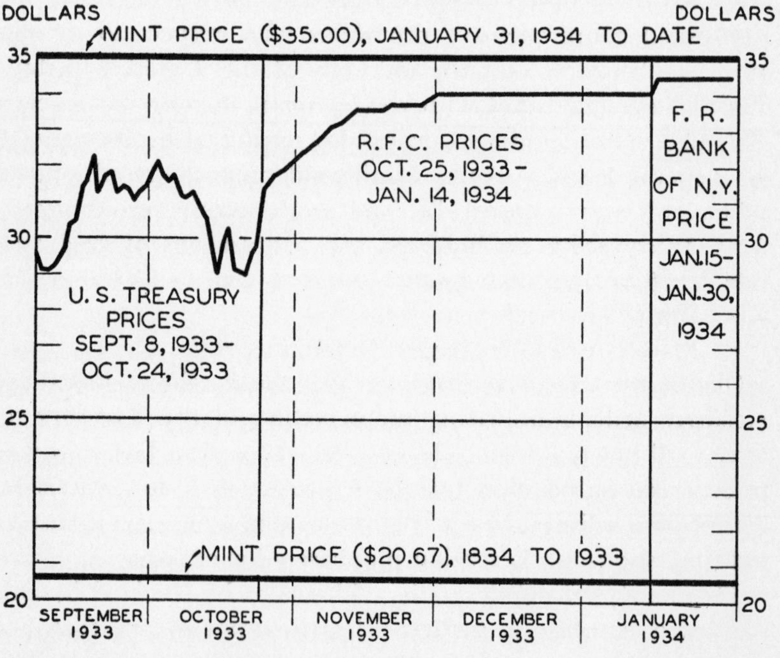

Source: United States Treasury Department.

stored "we shall seek to establish and maintain a dollar which will not change its purchasing and debt-paying power during the succeeding generation." He stated, also, that "our dollar is now altogether too greatly influenced by the accidents of international trade, by the internal policies of other nations, and by political disturbances in other continents. Therefore the United States must take firmly in its own hands the control of the gold value of our dollar. This is necessary in order to prevent dollar disturbances from swinging us away from our ultimate goal, namely, the continued recovery of our commodity prices."

The primary objective, hence, was to raise domestic prices to a satisfactory level. Following this, and contingent upon it, the Government would attempt purchasing-power stabilization as well as currency stabilization. To accomplish the primary aim, the President stated that he was about to establish a Government market for gold in the United States. He authorized the Reconstruction Finance Corporation to buy newly mined domestic gold at prices to be determined from time to time after consultation with the Secretary of the Treasury and the President. When necessary to consummate the end in view, the Reconstruction Finance Corporation would also buy and sell gold in the world market. The President stated this to be "a policy and not an expedient," and not a temporary move, but a move "toward a managed currency," and that "Government credit will be maintained and a sound currency will accompany a rise in the American price level."

In an executive order, issued October 25, 1933, the President amended the executive order of August 28, and revoked that of August 29, which had authorized the Secretary of the Treasury to sell newly mined domestic gold. The latest order authorized the Reconstruction Finance Corporation instead to be the buying and selling agency. The Corporation was permitted to acquire, hold, earmark for foreign account, export, or otherwise dispose of the gold.

Also on October 25, the Reconstruction Finance Corporation announced that it would issue notes, series of February 1, 1934, payment for which was to be received in gold. The total of notes offered at first amounted to $50,000,000, or thereabouts, and the notes were bearer obligations of the Reconstruction Finance Corporation and were to be fully and unconditionally guaranteed by the United States. They were issued on a discount basis at the rate of $\frac{1}{4}$ percent per annum, and would mature on February 1, 1934, 99 days after the Reconstruction Finance Corporation announcement.

Under the new policy, Government purchase of newly mined domestic gold was begun on October 25, at the rate of $31.36 per fine ounce. (See Chart II.) On October 30 purchases were extended to foreign markets at a rate of $31.96. The buying price continued upward almost unabated until December 1, when it reached $34.01, at which price it was maintained during the first half of the month. On December 18 the price was raised to $34.06, and this price obtained until January 15, 1934, when these operations were transferred to the Federal Reserve Bank of New York. The gold received by the Reconstruction Finance Corporation ranged in price from $31.36 to $34.06, and averaged, according to Treasury computations, $33.59 per fine ounce. It should be noted, in passing, that the purchasing prices quoted by the Reconstruction Finance Corporation did not apply to domestic gold other than that newly mined. Any other gold had to be turned in, and at a price of $20.67, the mint redemption price.

Subsequent to the initial steps taken in the Government's new gold policy under which the Reconstruction Finance Corporation purchased gold, nothing of significance occurred until December 28, 1933. On that date the executive order of August 28 was supplemented by an order of the Secretary of the Treasury requiring all gold coin, gold bullion, and gold certificates to be delivered for the account of the Treasurer of the United States. The Secretary's order required "every person subject to the jurisdiction of the United States, to deliver to the Treasurer of the United States all gold coin, gold bullion, and gold certificates situated in the United States," with certain stated exceptions: gold held under license; rare and unusual coins (excluding quarter eagles, or $2.50 pieces); gold held by the Federal Reserve Banks or the Reconstruction Finance Corporation; unmelted scrap gold, or gold sweepings up to $100, belonging to any one person; and fabricated gold.

An order of the Secretary of the Treasury was issued on January 15, 1934, in which he extended the time during which gold coin, bullion, and certificates could be turned over to the Government without penalty. This was but one more step in the long line of threats, pleadings, and cajolings invoked by the Administration during 1933 to persuade holders of any form of gold to turn it in at the Treasury.

On January 15, 1934, too, the Federal Reserve Bank of New York, acting as fiscal agent for the Treasury, began purchasing newly mined domestic gold for the mints and assay offices. This gold was paid for by a special issue of Treasury obligations dated January 16, 1934, and maturing on April 16, 1934; they bore an interest rate of $\frac{3}{8}$ths of one percent. On January 16 the price of gold was set at $34.45. (See Chart II.) It remained there until the end of the month, when President Roosevelt, under authority of the Gold Reserve Act of 1934, revalued the gold stock of the country at $35.00 per fine ounce.

THE PRESIDENT'S GOLD MESSAGE

Also on January 15, 1934, the President sent his special monetary message to Congress, asking for powers to revalue the gold dollar, nationalize gold, establish an exchange stabilization fund, and revert to a modified gold standard. In brief outline the message stated:

a. In conformity with the purpose of stabilizing the purchasing power of the dollar the President asks for "certain additional legislation to improve our financial and monetary system."

b. "The free circulation of gold coins is unnecessary, leads to hoarding, and tends to a possible weakening of national financial structures in times of emergency." Hence, transfer of gold within a country is "not only unnecessary but is in every way undesirable," and is "essential only for the payment of international trade balances."

c. Title and possession of all monetary gold within the United States should be vested in the Government, to hold in bullion rather than coin.

d. Although the President, under existing law, can order these actions, their importance make specific congressional sanction desirable.

e. While the present lower limit to revaluation is 50 percent, there should be set an upper limit at 60 percent of the present weight.

f. The Secretary of the Treasury should be given power to deal in gold and foreign exchange, at home and abroad. Of the devaluation profits, $2,000,000,000 should be set up as a special fund for these purposes.

g. No recommendation is to be made "looking to further extension of the monetary use of silver," until more is known of the effects on silver accruing from the London Conference Agreement and subsequent measures.

The message ended with the enunciation of "two principles." The first stressed a sound and adequate currency, with a fairly constant standard of purchasing power. The second principle was "the inherent right of government to issue currency and to be the sole custodian and owner of the base or reserve of precious metals underlying that currency."

THE GOLD RESERVE ACT OF 1934

The Congress complied with the President's requests and on January 30, 1934, presented to him for approval what became, upon his signing it, the Gold Reserve Act of 1934.[4]

---

[4] Following is a brief summary of the Act:

Purposes
   (1) To protect the currency system of the United States
   (2) To provide for the better use of the monetary gold stock
   (3) To withdraw gold from circulation
   (4) To stabilize monetary values

Measures to be taken to achieve the purposes
   (1) Title to all gold coin and bullion shall be vested in the United States and in payment therefor equivalent credits are established in the Treasury, balances in such accounts to be payable in gold certificates
   (2) The Secretary of the Treasury, with Presidential approval, shall prescribe conditions under which gold may be acquired, held, treated, imported, exported, or earmarked for industrial or artistic uses, for the settling of international balances, or for other purposes not inconsistent with the stated objects of the act
   (3) Gold coinage is discontinued except that for foreign countries; all gold coin is to be withdrawn and melted into ingots and redemption in gold is prohibited except in connection with Federal Reserve transactions deemed necessary by the Secretary of the Treasury to maintain equal purchasing power; and such redemption is to be in gold bullion
   (4) A $2,000,000,000 stabilization fund is to be set up under the control of the Secretary of the Treasury, subject to review by the President only

As a first step in the execution of the Act, title to all gold coin and bullion in the Federal Reserve System was transferred to the United States Government, in exchange for equivalent dollar credits in the United States Treasury. This transfer vested in the United States all right, title, and interest and every claim of the Federal Reserve Board, the Federal Reserve Banks, and the Federal Reserve Agents to all gold coin and bullion. In payment, at $20.67 per ounce, the Treasury established credits on its books in equivalent amounts in dollars. These credits were payable in gold certificates. Gold held by the Federal Reserve Board, the Federal Reserve Banks, and the Federal Reserve Agents was required to be held in custody for the United States and delivered upon order of the Secretary of the Treasury.

All gold coins of the United States were to be withdrawn from circulation. These coins and any other gold owned by the United States Government were to be formed into bars. No gold was to be minted thereafter.

The redemption of currency in gold was prohibited, except as allowed by regulations of the Secretary of the Treasury with the approval of the President, and then only in gold bullion. Gold certificates owned by the Federal Reserve Banks were to be redeemable at such amounts as in the judgment of the Secretary of the Treasury were necessary "to maintain the equal purchasing power of every kind of currency of the United States." Such redemptions too were to be made only in gold bullion.

The Act also provided that the reserve for the United States notes and for the Treasury notes of 1890 was to be maintained in gold bullion equal to the dollar amounts required by law.

The Secretary of the Treasury was given the authority to buy or sell gold as an operation in the General Fund of the Treasury, at such rates and upon such terms and conditions as

---

(5) The weight of the gold dollar may be fixed at not more than 60 percent and not less than 50 percent of its present (January 30, 1934) weight

(6) The President is authorized to issue silver certificates and to reduce the weight of silver coin in the same proportion as he may reduce the gold dollar.

he deemed most advantageous to the public interest. But gold held as currency reserve or security could be sold only to the extent necessary to maintain the currency at a parity with the gold dollar. The Secretary of the Treasury was also authorized to deal in gold and foreign exchange and such other instruments of credit and securities as he deemed necessary for stabilizing the exchange value of the dollar. A stabilization fund of $2,000,000,000 was to be established for this purpose out of the increment resulting from the reduction in the weight of the gold dollar.

Another main provision of the Gold Reserve Act amended Title III of the Act of May 12, 1933, stating that in the re-weighting of the gold dollar the new weight should not be fixed at more than 60 percent of the weight then existing.[5] Thus, this re-wording set the upper and lower limits at which the weight of the new dollar could be fixed at 50 and 60 percent of the then existing weight of the dollar. That is, it permitted the price of gold to be changed from $20.67 per ounce, nine-tenths fine, to any price between $41.34 and $34.45 per ounce.

THE DEVALUATION PROCLAMATION

On January 31, 1934, President Roosevelt issued a proclamation revaluing the gold dollar by reducing the amount of gold in the dollar to 59.06 percent of its former content. That is, he lowered the gold content of the dollar from 25.8 grains of gold nine-tenths fine to 15 5/21 ounces nine-tenths fine, or in other words, he raised the value of gold from $20.67 per fine ounce, to $35.00 per fine ounce. (See heavy lines in Chart II, indicating mint gold price.) However, he also reserved "the right to alter or modify this proclamation as the interest of the United States may seem to require." The proclamation was issued at 3:10 P. M. on January 31. The Daily Treasury Statement of that date stated that the books had been closed as of 3:00 o'clock P. M., so that the amount of "profit" from this de-

---

[5] "The authority contained in title III of the act of May 12, 1933, permitting the President under certain conditions to fix the weight of the gold dollar at not less than 50 percent of its then legal weight, was made more specific by adding the provision that the weight of the gold dollar shall not be fixed at more than 60 percent of its then legal weight." Secretary of the Treasury, *Annual Report*, 1934, p. 28.

weighting was not shown in the Treasury Statement until the next day, February 1, 1934. The main reason for delaying the proclamation was undoubtedly to wait until that time of the day when the financial markets were closed, both here and abroad, and thus avoid any upsetting of their situations. This would also give them opportunity to become adjusted before opening the next day. The gold market, however, would still be open at that time.

The mints were authorized to purchase (a) gold recovered from natural deposits in the United States or any place subject to the jurisdiction thereof, which had not entered into monetary or industrial use, (b) unmelted scrap gold, and (c) gold imported into the United States after January 30, 1934. Purchases and sales were to be made at the rate of $35 per fine troy ounce, not including a handling charge of ¼ percent and the usual mint charges. This price, however, could be changed by the Secretary of the Treasury without notice other than by notice of such change mailed or telegraphed to the mints.

The United States Treasury Daily Statement of February 1st, under the caption "Receipts—Miscellaneous," showed an item titled "Increment resulting from reduction in the weight of the gold dollar, $2,805,512,060.87." On February 28, 1934, this item was removed from the "General and Special Funds" account of the Daily Treasury Statement, to the "Trust, and Contributed Funds and Increment on Gold" account. From February 1, 1934, to the end of 1937, only $10,000,000 additional "profit" was reported on this score.

Total "profit" by the end of 1937 thus amounted to $2,816,-000,000. It was disposed of as follows: $2,000,000,000 to the exchange stabilization fund; $645,000,000 towards the redemption of national bank notes; $27,000,000 to the Federal Reserve Banks for making industrial loans; $2,000,000 charged off to melting losses; and, $141,000,000 still remaining in the general fund cash balance.

FURTHER GOLD RESTRICTIONS

On the day that President Roosevelt de-weighted the gold dollar, the Secretary of the Treasury issued regulations, under the Gold Reserve Act, which made even tighter the restrictions on the acquisition, transportation, melting or treatment, earmarking, and import or export of gold. Federal Reserve Banks were authorized to acquire gold bullion from the United States by redemption of gold certificates in such amounts as, "in the judgment of the Secretary of the Treasury," were necessary to settle international balances or to maintain the equal purchasing power of every kind of currency of the United States.

The Secretary of the Treasury also stated that whenever exchange rates with gold standard currencies should reach the gold export point he would sell gold for export to foreign central banks at the rate of $35 per fine troy ounce plus a handling charge of ¼ percent. The exports were to be made only to foreign central banks buying and selling gold at fixed prices. Most of the purchases of imported gold, as well as sales of gold for export were to be made through the Federal Reserve Bank of New York as fiscal agent of the United States.

THE EXCHANGE STABILIZATION FUND

A section of the Gold Reserve Act provided that, of the gold dollar devaluation "profit," $2,000,000,000 was to be set up as a stabilization fund. This fund was to be under the exclusive control of the Secretary of the Treasury, subject only to the approval of the President. It was to be available for expenditure for the purpose of stabilizing the exchange value of the dollar. Also, any portion of the fund not currently required for stabilizing the exchange value of the dollar was available for investing in direct obligations of the United States.

The $2,000,000,000 was not so earmarked until the United States Treasury Daily Statement of April 27, 1934, when there appeared for the first time the item "Chargeable against increment on gold: Exchange stabilization fund, $2,000,000,-000.00." However, of the $2,000,000,000 set aside, only $200,-000,000 was put into a working fund, while $1,800,000,000 remained, and still remains (March, 1938), in the gold asset and liability statement as gold credited to the exchange stabilization fund. The $200,000,000 had been deposited, presumably, in a special account with the Federal Reserve Banks.

The workings of the fund were to be shrouded in complete secrecy, and on the whole such secrecy has been maintained. Only twice was there any break in the wall of silence. A French finance minister publicly thanked Secretary Morgenthau for aiding the French franc through the stabilization fund, and Secretary Morgenthau's embarrassment was undeniable. In the autumn of 1936, Secretary Morgenthau himself gave out some information on the operations of the fund. This occurred the day after the tripartite agreement, in which had appeared the statement that the United States "trusts that no country will attempt to obtain an unreasonable competitive exchange advantage and thereby hamper the effort to restore more stable economic relations." On September 26, Secretary Morgenthau purchased £1,000,000 offered by Russia, in order to halt what Treasury officials thought at first was an attempt by Russia to drive down sterling, and also to serve notice that the United States would go the limit to protect the monetary and exchange equilibrium sought by the agreement. Later in the day the officials changed their minds as to the motive of Russia, and on following days were roundly denounced by the press for magnifying a small, routine deal.

It might be mentioned in passing that, following upon the passage of the Gold Reserve Act, the monetary inflationists shifted their strategy to silver, and for the next year or two silver held the center of the monetary and inflation stage. Discussion of this phase of the monetary policies of the United States appears in Chapter III, below.

THE SUPREME COURT DECISIONS UPHOLDING THE GOLD-CLAUSE ABROGATION

Little other Administration action of significance occurred as regards gold in the two and one-half years following the passage of the Gold Reserve Act, except for the gold-clause decisions of the Supreme Court on February 18, 1935. These decisions upheld almost completely the gold-clause abrogation law of June 5, 1933. These were, of course, not directly activities of the Administration, but rather were judicial confirmation of some of those activities.

The passage of a law on August 27, 1935, providing for the exchange of gold-clause obligations, was but supplementary to previous actions taken with respect to gold, and was consequent upon the Supreme Court decisions. This law entitled the lawful holders of coins or currencies of the United States to exchange them, dollar for dollar, for other coins or currencies which could be lawfully acquired.

Also, for a limited period, this law entitled the owners of the gold-clause securities of the United States, including those not yet due, to receive immediate payment of the stated dollar amount thereof with interest to the date of payment or to prior maturity or to prior redemption date, whichever was earlier. The period within which the owners of gold-clause securities were entitled to receive payment prior to maturity was to expire January 1, 1936, or on such later date, not after July 1, 1936, as might be fixed by the Secretary of the Treasury. Pursuant to the authority of this law, regulations, approved by the President on September 14, 1935, were issued governing the immediate payment of outstanding gold-clause securities and the exchange of coins and currencies of the United States.

The Act stated, too, that after January 1, 1936, the consent of the United States to be sued "upon any gold-clause securities or for interest thereon, or upon any coin or currency, or upon any claim arising out of requisition of such coin or currency, or of any gold or silver, and involving the effect or validity of any change in the metallic content of the dollar, or other regulation of the value of money," was withdrawn. Furthermore, no authorized appropriation would be available for payment except on an equal dollar-for-dollar basis.

THE GOLD DELUGE

The price of $35.00 per ounce set for gold by President Roosevelt on January 31, 1934, proved a magnet for a large part of the world's gold.[6] The steady stream of gold imports

[6] "The new rate for the dollar greatly undervalued this currency. This had the effect not only of encouraging a heavy inflow of capital to participate in the expected rise of values in this market, but also of intensifying the economic difficulties of the gold bloc countries and so contributing to a flight of capital from them. The result was a heavy demand for dollars in excess of the supply, with consequent depression of exchange rates to levels promoting gold imports." National City Bank, *Monthly Letter*, November 1935, p. 168.

into the United States during the succeeding four years amounted, in all, to well over $5,000,000,000. (See Charts I and III.) This attraction of the monetary reserves of other nations cannot be ascribed entirely to the high price set for the metal in the United States, but was due in part also to the establishment of a fixed value for gold, at least for the time being. In addition, the recurring war scares and the political upheavals on the continent were also instrumental in sending frightened gold to the United States. Other factors responsible

Chart III

MONETARY GOLD STOCK OF THE UNITED STATES

(At End of Each Month)

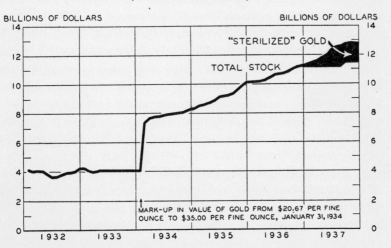

Sources: United States Treasury Department; Board of Governors of the Federal Reserve System.

for the inflow of gold to the United States include the increased sale of merchandise abroad, and the inflow of capital into the United States. Part of this capital inflow reflected a return of American funds which had been transferred abroad in 1933. The rest of it was foreign-owned capital sent here either to build up dollar balances or to purchase American securities.

Some have uttered fears that this pouring of gold into the United States may ultimately make this nation a dumping-ground for a commodity which will eventually lose its monetary value. It is claimed that the scarcity, or rather complete absence, of gold in the monetary and central bank reserves of a number of nations cannot help but force them to leave gold definitely and permanently. It would be hard to believe that such a situation could ever come to pass. No nation, even of those most rabidly management-minded as regards their currencies, has ever lost its desire to obtain and hold gold in its monetary reserves. All the hindrances to international trade, all the defense measures set up, such as tariff increases to offset currency depreciation of other nations, the imposition of quotas and embargoes, anti-dumping laws, sumptuary regulations, extreme sanitary regulations, exchange restrictions, blocked currencies, bilateral trade treaties, clearing agreements, and the like, all are strongly indicative of the very active presence of that desire.

THE TRIPARTITE AGREEMENT, SEPTEMBER, 1936

The revaluation of the gold dollar on January 31, 1934, and the regulations of the Secretary of the Treasury permitting the sale as well as purchase of gold under certain conditions, stabilized the United States dollar and returned us to a *de facto* gold standard of a limited sort. This situation obtained until the autumn of 1936, when the French Government was experiencing fiscal and monetary difficulties. Partly as a face-saving device for that Government and partly because it was driven by necessity, when Premier Blum attempted to "reflate" the French economy after Premier Laval's apparently disastrous and violent attempt at "deflating" it, the French Government held conversations with Great Britain and the United States. On September 25, 1936, the United States Secretary of the Treasury, by authority of the President, issued a statement similar to statements issued on the same day by the Governments of Great Britain and France.

The points in the statement are outlined as follows:

(1) The United States, Great Britain and France look to measures to promote world prosperity, improve the standard of living, and safeguard peace.

(2) The United States, like the others, in its policy toward in-

ternational monetary relations, must "take into full account the requirements of internal prosperity."

(3) The French government admits the "need" to propose to its Parliament "the readjustment of its currency." The United States and Great Britain welcome this decision. All three nations will try to avoid any disturbance that might result.

(4) Success depends upon the development of international trade. The United States hopes for the relaxing and the ultimate abolition of quotas and exchange control.

(5) An invitation is made to other nations to join, and the hope is expressed that none tries to obtain an "unreasonable competitive exchange advantage" and thus hinder future "stable economic relations, which it is the aim of the three governments to promote."

This "gentlemen's agreement" was practically nothing but words. It merely served as a stop-gap to the adverse criticism which would undoubtedly have been leveled at Premier Blum had he attempted to devalue the French franc without first persuading his people that it was part of a process of "readjustment" engaged in simultaneously by the "three great democracies," in their effort to stabilize the world's currency and political situations.

The gentlemen's tripartite agreement did not restore the gold standard in the three countries. Indeed, it did not restore or set up any standard. It did not say that gold is the foundation upon which the currencies are to be based. In fact it left the situation so wide open that paper money, silver, commodities, and indeed almost anything might be used as the basis upon which stability was to be effected.

Furthermore, the agreement was set up on a 24-hour footing, and each nation, in its policy towards international monetary relations, was not to relinquish anything which would threaten its internal prosperity.

It is difficult to see how three stabilization funds, based upon three radically different internal monetary systems, could effect the stabilization of the international monetary systems of these nations. The United States exchange stabilization fund, which was created out of the "profits" resulting from the reduction in the weight of the gold dollar, was alleged to have as its primary function the stabilization of the American dollar at home and abroad, at \$35.00 per fine ounce. The British exchange equalization account, set up and financed by Treasury bills, was to stabilize the pound sterling, or rather to keep the pound sterling from fluctuating too much. But what was to constitute too much and what point of reference was to be used, were not described. The French stabilization fund, like the American, also was set up from devaluation "profits." It was supposed to keep the franc from fluctuating outside the range of 66 to 75 percent of the gold value set by the monetary law of June 25, 1928.

Thus, there were a presumably fixed American currency, a wholly free British currency, and an intermediate French one neither fixed nor yet movable in any large degree. By the device of three equalization or stabilization funds, these three diverse and widely unlike currency situations were to be stabilized, not only in themselves but also relative to one another. The collapse of the French franc in June, 1937, attested to the frailness of this arrangement, despite the meaningless lip service paid to the tripartite agreement by the French politicians.

THE SECOND SUSPENSION OF THE GOLD STANDARD

On October 12, 1936, the United States, after being on a limited *de facto* gold standard for almost three years, left that standard. This was effected by the comparatively simple procedure outlined in the Treasury press release of that date. That release stated that the United States would sell gold for immediate export to, or earmark for the account of, the exchange equalization or stabilization funds of those countries which would do likewise for the United States. Such sale would be effected only if terms, conditions and rates were satisfactory to the Secretary as being "most advantageous to the public interest." All sales were to be through the Federal Reserve Bank of New York, at the rate of \$35.00 per fine ounce, with a one-quarter of one percent handling charge. Daily announcements were promised of the nations complying with the provisions, and therefore eligible to participate in this buying and selling game. On October 12, 1936, Great Britain and France were listed as complying.

Thus the tripartite agreement succeeded in taking the United States off its limited gold standard and made this country a coöperating party in the English and French currency manipulations.

A month or so later the Secretary of the Treasury supplemented his October 12 announcement. He stated on November 23, 1936, that the United States would sell gold for immediate export to, or earmark for account of, not only exchange equalization or stabilization funds, but also "the treasuries, or any fiscal agencies acting for or whose acts in this connection are guaranteed by the treasuries." This announcement too applied only to countries which would reciprocate, and only if terms and conditions were satisfactory to the Secretary as being "most advantageous to the public interest." Belgium, the Netherlands, and Switzerland[7] were added to the list of those nations "complying," and eligible to buy gold from the United States.

On that day the Secretary announced further that his statement of January 31, 1934, relating to the sale of gold for export, was "accordingly withdrawn." This meant presumably that gold could not be exported to settle international balances, but could be sold only to the complying nations.

Incidentally, it should be noted that the international currency game indulged in by the presumably democratic countries was being played behind walls of strict secrecy. The rules of this game, as well as the moves, were known to a few insiders only. It does not seem conformable to democratic principles that a nation's most vital matters be kept from the populace making up that nation.

GOLD "STERILIZATION"

A problem raised by the enormous influx of gold into the United States was the fact that it increased the volume of excess reserves, thus creating inflationary possibilities too great to view

[7] The difficulties of France in September and October, 1936, were reflected in Switzerland and Holland, and when they too left gold, the "gold bloc" as an entity ceased to exist.

serenely. Consequently, after our monetary gold stock had risen in three years by more than $4,000,000,000, the Treasury decided to halt the inflationary potentialities of any further gold increase in the monetary stock by "offsetting" or "sterilizing" it. Beginning on December 24, 1936, gold purchases by the Treasury were placed in an "inactive" account, and instead of issuing gold certificates in payment, which could serve as the base for note and credit expansion, the Treasury, in effect, paid out its own obligations.[8] By the end of 1937, the Treasury had placed more than $1,000,000,000 in its "inactive" fund (see Chart III), and was paying interest on that amount of debt to keep the gold sterile. The costliness of such a program, as well as its apparent futility in stemming inflationary potentialities, rapidly became apparent. But the ready remedy—reducing the price of gold—was politically too dangerous to use, even though it was economically desirable, and even though the Secretary of the Treasury could vary the purchase price of foreign gold without changing its domestic monetary value.[9] The inflationary bloc in Congressional and Administration circles—still potent, as evidenced by recurrent bills to depreciate the currency even more—prevented the taking of any such economically sound step.

The "sterilization" procedure was looked upon generally with favor as preventing any further increase in excess reserves, and thus as heading off an incipient credit inflation. This was especially important in view of the prospect of continued gold inflow, not only because of the high price obtainable in the United States, which is the only nation willing to take at a fixed price all the gold offered, but also because of the international economic and political outlook, which was still dis-

[8] "The Secretary of the Treasury, after conferring with the Board of Governors of the Federal Reserve System, announces that he proposes, whenever it is deemed advisable and in the public interest to do so, to take appropriate action with respect to net additional acquisitions or releases of gold by the Treasury Department.

"This will be accomplished by the sale of additional public debt obligations, the proceeds of which will be used for the purchase of gold, and by the purchase or redemption of outstanding obligations in the case of movements in the reverse direction." United States Treasury Press Release No. 9–20, December 21, 1936.

[9] As set by the Presidential Proclamation of January 31, 1934.

turbed. The step was also regarded as a safeguard to our credit system if and when the gold should later be drained back abroad. The Treasury was commended for its policy of keeping the nation informed on the size of the "inactive" gold account, instead of holding that information secret too.[10]

Apart from the objection to the cost of the program, only one other real fault was found. That was that the operation was simply one more step in the direction of Government-controlled credit.

It might be mentioned in passing that this so-called gold "sterilization" procedure could have been applied equally well to any other form of money. For example, the Treasury might have issued say $2,000,000,000 in securities and demanded only Federal Reserve notes in payment, which it could then bury in a special "inactive" fund. In this way too, then, as in the case of gold "sterilization," the Treasury would be issuing securities to sop up from the money market funds that might otherwise serve to bolster a credit inflation.

The "sterilization" operations were precisely analogous in effects to the recent increases in the required reserves of member banks.[11] That is, in the Treasury "sterilization" operations the Treasury salts away, as it were, whatever new gold becomes available, thus preventing the increase in the credit base which this gold could effect. By increasing required reserve ratios, the Board of Governors of the Federal Reserve System, in effect, orders the member banks to salt away some of their funds and thus refrain from using them as a basis for credit expansion.

In July, 1937, the United States Treasury entered into two agreements by which it would be enabled to get rid of some of its gold surplus. On July 9, announcement was made of arrangements again to sell gold to China in order to enable her to augment her gold reserve, and in exchange we were to re-

---

[10] On February 14, 1938, the Secretary of the Treasury announced a modification in the "sterilization" program. Gold acquired after January 1, 1938, was to be sterilized only to the extent that it exceeded $100,000,000 in any one quarter. Thus, gold acquisitions up to that amount would be permitted to swell the credit base and increase the volume of member bank reserves.

[11] In three successive steps, effective August 15, 1936, March 1, 1937, and May 1, 1937, the required reserve ratios of member banks were made double those formerly prescribed in the Federal Reserve Act.

ceive silver. On July 16, an agreement was announced by which the United States was to sell up to $60,000,000 worth of gold to Brazil. One of the purposes was stated to be "to promote the development of conditions favorable to the maintenance of monetary equilibrium between the two countries."

SUMMARY

In brief summary, the gold policy of the United States consisted of a series of measures which "nationalized" gold, raised its price, fostered an increase in its production, and reburied it. The losses of gold to foreign countries in late 1931 and most of 1932 induced an acute monetary and credit stringency in the United States. By March, 1933, as the Roosevelt Administration took office, the financial machinery of the nation was tottering and panic-stricken. The strong measures undertaken by the incoming Administration bolstered up the system for a time. In the process, though, the Administration succeeded in seizing complete control of the gold and monetary machinery.

Domestically owned gold was called in, coins were melted into bullion, and all gold, imported and newly mined, was purchased by the Government. The large increase in the monetary gold stock, and the threat of impending inflation, gave rise to fears as to the stability of the credit machinery should a boom develop. Consequently, the Treasury, by gold "sterilization," attempted to offset, in some part, the inflationary effects of the increase in the gold stock.

The Board of Governors of the Federal Reserve System contributed their share in effecting monetary control by doubling the reserve ratios of its member banks. Also, the insistent demand by the Federal Deposit Insurance Corporation that banks increase their capital before enlarging their loan portfolios, was also a step in the direction of halting the feared inflation.

However, the recession in the autumn of 1937 induced the monetary authorities to call a halt in their "deflationary" steps. Consequently, in September the Treasury "desterilized" $300,-000,000 of its gold. Also, in November, the Federal Reserve Banks resorted to the purchase of Governments in the open market.

At the end of 1937 the gold policy of the Administration was still in a state of flux. Persistent rumors as to further devaluation, and apparently substantial Congressional support for it, give rise to more fears. We are still left with the question: How much further is the Administration going in its groping about for an economically sound gold policy?

III

"DOING SOMETHING" FOR SILVER

THE silver interests should be very grateful to the "New Deal" Administration, which early showed its zeal toward "doing something for silver." An Administration which succeeds in raising the price of silver from about $0.25 per fine ounce to around $0.80, in the short space of two years, gives the silver miners and speculators much for which to be thankful. Also, the increased general interest in a commodity in which such interest had been dull or entirely lacking[1] could not prove displeasing to the silver people. Of course, the slight drop in the following two years in the market price of silver to $0.45 per fine ounce did set them back a little. But even that was a figure almost twice the depression low for silver prices reached in December, 1932. Furthermore, newly mined domestic silver obtained, until recently, almost $0.78 per fine ounce from the Government. Its price was reduced, on January 1, 1938, to $0.6464.

It is true that the Administration, in its eagerness to satisfy the silver interests, may have been a little over-zealous in its endeavors. It did force China off the silver standard, and did cause difficulty to other silver-using nations. Also, the vigor with which it carried out its mandate may have put an end to one of silver's most important markets for the future. Still the Government did give the industry immediately higher prices, and with that main objective fulfilled, any drawbacks likely to occur in the future can be dismissed as but slight offsets and need not be worried about until they do take place.

[1] "The year 1932 appeared destined to be recorded as an uneventful one from the standpoint of silver, because a featureless market had prevailed for nearly eleven months and no change from existing conditions was expected. But this view proved mistaken, and silver history was written when the New York market sank to new record lows during the last week of November and again in December.

"On December 29th a record low price of 24¼¢ for the white metal was quoted, and 1932 closed with the market only ⅛¢ higher. Large stocks of silver were on hand in the various trading centers of the world at the end of the year." Handy and Harman, *Annual Review*, 1932, pp. 1, 5, 6.

"THOMAS" INFLATION AMENDMENT AND SILVER

The Government first definitely showed its interest in silver when, in the "Thomas" Amendment to the Act of May 12, 1933, there appeared a provision which permitted silver to be fixed in any ratio to gold, whenever the President found such action necessary to stabilize domestic prices or to protect the foreign commerce of the United States against the adverse effects of depreciated foreign currencies. This gave the President *carte blanche* to proceed to put the United States on a free silver basis. Another section of the "Thomas" Amendment made silver, along with all other currencies, legal tender.

Still a third section also related to silver. That section permitted silver to be received, within the six months following the passage of the Act, in payment of the debts of foreign Governments owed to the United States Government and at the rate of $0.50 per fine ounce, a value almost twice the going market price at the time. The President was authorized to accept silver in payment of the whole or any part of the principal or interest due within those six months. The maximum amount which could be received under this provision was limited to $200,000,000, or 400,000,000 ounces. The amount actually received however, was but 22,734,824.35 ounces, which at $0.50 per fine ounce, was worth $11,367,412.18.

The following table, prepared by the United States Treasury, shows the nations which took advantage of the provision, and the extent to which they did so. (See also Chart V.)

SILVER PAYMENTS RECEIVED FROM FOREIGN GOVERNMENTS ON ACCOUNT OF AMOUNTS DUE JUNE 15, 1933

Country	Fine Ounces	Value at 50 Cents an Ounce
Czechoslovakia	359,010.49	$179,505.25
Finland	296,631.88	148,315.94
Great Britain	20,001,036.84	10,000,518.42
Italy	2,000,041.52	1,000,020.76
Lithuania	19,980.70	9,990.35
Rumania	58,122.92	29,061.46
	22,734,824.35	$11,367,412.18

Seemingly, foreign governments did not think it worth while to take the opportunity offered to discharge a portion of their debt to the United States. There was probably no reason why they should, when they knew that the debts, so far as they were concerned, were practically a dead issue anyway.

Such debt receipts proved of little benefit to domestic producers. In fact, the reaction on the New York silver market was unfavorable, and a price decline took place. However, some other factors contributed to the decline, especially the resolution presented by Senator Pittman to the Monetary Commission of the London Economic Conference. Although that resolution was aimed to benefit silver in a direct manner, as is explained below, it also set international currency stabilization, and on a gold basis, as the primary aim of the Conference.

REMONETIZATION OF SILVER

The next step directly affecting silver was taken in connection with the Resolution of June 5, 1933, which abrogated the gold clause from all contracts,[2] and made all forms of United States coins and currency legal tender for all debts, public and private, past and future. Included, of course, were silver coins and silver certificates. The repetition of the provisions from the "Thomas" Amendment making all coins and currencies legal tender was probably necessary to soothe the doubts and misgivings in the minds of some of the legislators and administrators after the passage of the "Thomas" Amendment.

LONDON ECONOMIC CONFERENCE

The opening of the World Economic Conference at London on June 12, 1933, gave the Administration another opportunity to show its concern over silver. Mainly upon the insistence of the United States delegate, Senator Key Pittman, the leading silver-producing and silver-using nations of the world were persuaded to enter into an agreement under which they promised to take and keep excess silver off the world's markets, limit its unrestricted sale, and increase its monetary use. The purpose, of course, was to enhance the price of silver. Senator Pittman had already cultivated the ground and merely harvested, at the Conference, the maturing fruits of his toil. For, as far back

[2] See *supra*, p. 19.

as February, he had announced the President's approval of his objective of raising the price of silver through the Conference. Then in May, he said that all the countries to the Conference had agreed "in principle" on plans to rehabilitate silver. At the same time, the President of the United States and the Finance Ministers of China and Mexico issued joint statements from Washington indicating that they were favorably disposed toward such rehabilitation.

The anomaly of Senator Pittman's position at the Conference, at which he advocated the gold standard and international currency stabilization while working hard for silver, is made evident by the following quotation:

After the first two points of Mr. Pittman's resolution covering the re-establishment of the gold standard and international currency stabilization had been unanimously adopted on June 20th by the Monetary Commission, with an amendment permitting each country to decide when and at what parity its currency should be stabilized, the balance of this resolution was referred to sub-committees. The Silver Sub-Committee, over which Senator Pittman presided, was allotted the task of formulating an agreement by which silver should be accredited greater use for national monetary reserves and subsidiary coinage, and by which co-operation in the matter of sales should be secured between those countries which are large producers, and those which are large holders of silver.[3]

The deliberations concerning silver caused wide fluctuations in the world markets. In the early stages of the sub-committee's talks, the apparently unfavorable progress induced some selling and a consequent decline in the market. Then when it was thought that the Conference was on the verge of collapse over the question of monetary stabilization, silver fell again. However, President Roosevelt's message of July 2 resulted in a decision by the Steering Committee to continue the Conference. This gave renewed hope to the "silverites."

Reports during the second week of July that a silver agreement had been accepted indicated substantial progress towards silver stabilization on the basis of an accord between India to limit its sales of metal and the producing countries to absorb

[3] Handy and Harman, *Annual Review*, 1933, p. 13.

a compensating amount in their treasuries. Spain was said to be desirous of selling a certain percentage of its Central Bank silver reserves, and decisions from Australia and Japan were pending; and it was announced that the acceptance in principle, by the leading nations concerned, strengthened the hope for ultimate agreement. This too caused increased buying.

INTERNATIONAL SILVER AGREEMENT

The results which emanated from the sub-committee and which were later adopted by the interested nations concerned raised a storm of protest. Especially stressed were the ulterior and insidious motives which were alleged to be behind the Agreement.[4]

Representatives of sixty-six governments were signatories to the first of the silver resolutions—that signed on July 20, 1933. This resolution provided that the governments would cease the debasement and demonetization of silver, substitute silver for small-denomination currency, and enact no legislation harmful to silver.

The more significant agreement was signed on July 22, and provided, in addition to the promises listed above, that the signatories would support the silver market. The agreement embodied a four-year silver control plan and was assented to by eight nations. The Governments of India, China, and Spain, as holders of large stocks of silver and as users of silver, promised to limit sales of silver, and the Governments of Australia, Canada, Mexico, Peru, and the United States, as principal producers of silver, agreed to absorb 35,000,000 ounces of silver annually. The operations subsequent to the agreement were to be maintained over the succeeding four years.

The annual amounts of silver to be purchased, withdrawn

---

[4] "The terms of this agreement lead inevitably to the conclusion that the seven other nations joining the United States in the compact were persuaded to sign it because it was without material significance for them and they could assent to the urgent request of a powerful nation without any economic consequence to themselves. The whole agreement was engineered for two purposes—to give support to the notion that silver is of international importance and to gild a scheme for a Congressional subsidy to silver with the color of an international compact." Neil Carothers, *Silver in America*, p. 19.

from or held off the market, or otherwise absorbed were as follows: [5]

1. Australia	652,365 fine ounces
2. Canada	1,672,802 fine ounces
3. Mexico	7,159,108 fine ounces
4. Peru	1,095,325 fine ounces
5. United States	24,472,410 fine ounces
Total	35,052,010 fine ounces

The limitations as to sales by the three large holders were as follows:

1. Indian Government sales limited to a total of 140,000,000 ounces for the four years commencing January 1, 1934, and not more than 50,000,000 ounces to be sold in any one year

2. Spanish Government sales limited to a total of 20,000,000 ounces, and the yearly maximum to be 7,000,000 ounces

3. Chinese Government sales of demonetized coins prohibited during this period

The agreement was scheduled to remain in force until January 1, 1938. While it was provided that the agreement would not be effective unless ratified by all the eight nations concerned on or before April 1, 1934, this provision was of no consequence. The reason is that even if any country should fail to ratify the compact, it would still be valid for those who did sign if they would agree to purchase the entire 35,000,000 ounces. This cunning maneuver to subsidize the American silver producer at the expense of the American Government (or taxpayer) is revealed in all its crudeness when it is pointed out that Mexico, producing twice as much silver as the United States, was listed to take less than one-third as much as this country. Indeed, the theoretical share of the United States was almost exactly equal to this country's total output in 1932, which amounted to 23,980,773 ounces.

The fact that the agreement was binding upon Governments proved of little moment a year or so later when it was possible to export silver to the United States at a handsome profit.[6] As the restrictions applied to Government sales only, they could

[5] United States Department of State, *Treaty Information*, Bulletin No. 47, August 31, 1933, pp. 12, 13, 18–21.
[6] See *infra*, p. 57.

not prevent silver shipments on private, commercial account. Also, the pious hopes uttered by the signers of the agreement as to the possibilities of increased trade were due to be blasted too.

RATIFICATION BY THE UNITED STATES

The President proclaimed ratification of the silver agreement on December 21, 1933, when he ordered the mints to be opened to the entire silver production of American miners during the four years ending December 31, 1937.

Chart IV

Silver Prices: Government Purchase Prices versus Open Market Price

(In Cents per Fine Ounce)

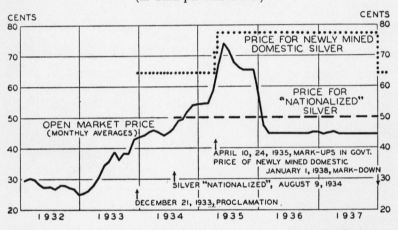

Sources: United States Treasury Department; *Survey of Current Business.*

The proclamation was issued under authority of the "Thomas" Inflation Amendment to the Act of May 12, 1933. By its terms, the mints were directed to accept, during the succeeding four years, any silver produced from natural deposits in the United States or in any place subject to its jurisdiction. Of the silver so tendered, the Director of the Mint, with the voluntary consent of the owner, was to pay the owner with standard silver dollars coined from 50 percent of the silver, or with similar silver dollars already coined. The other half of the tendered silver was a charge imposed by the Government for seigniorage and miscellaneous services undertaken in connection with such coinage. Furthermore, the silver retained by the Government was not to be disposed of before December 31, 1937, except in the form of United States coins.

The monetary value of silver at that time was $1.2929+$[7] per fine ounce. By deducting a seigniorage charge of 50 percent, the mint paid only $0.6464+$ per fine ounce. (See Chart IV.) The owner of the silver, however, had no cause for complaint as the transaction netted him a return almost half again as much as he could have obtained in the open market. Thus, the existence of an open-market price on the one hand, and of a governmental price on the other, really established two classifications for silver, one purchasable by the Government, the other in the open market by the trade. In effect, therefore, for some purposes it could be considered that there were two commodities called "silver," and not one.

Thus instead of the President's ordering the purchase of the quota amount, as set in the London silver agreement, he threw the mints open to the entire American output. United States production in 1932 averaged 2,000,000 ounces per month, and the price bounty offered by the Government could not help but stimulate production. The extent to which this turned out to be the case can readily be seen in Chart VIII. Indeed, by 1937, output had almost trebled the 1932 level.

INCREASED SUBSIDY

The domestic producer continued to receive, from the Treasury, $0.6464+$ per fine ounce during 1934 and the first three months of 1935. But, in April, 1935, due in part to the vigorous buying program of the United States Government under the Silver Purchase Act of 1934,[8] the world price of silver rose almost vertically and on April 26, 1935, reached a record figure of $0.8131. The Federal Government meanwhile had promised that it would not abandon the domestic producer, and on April 10, 1935, it lowered the seigniorage charge

---

[7] As it still is in April, 1938.
[8] See *infra*, p. 69, *et seq.*

from 50 percent to 45 percent, or, in other words, raised the price (net) to the domestic producer to $0.7111 per fine ounce.

World prices of silver still continued upward, and on April 24, 1935, the Administration again affirmed its decision to provide for the domestic producer. By lowering the seigniorage again, this time to 40 percent, it raised its purchase price for newly mined domestic silver by the same amount as before, that is, to $0.7757 per fine ounce. This price obtained through the remainder of the year, and until the end of 1937. On January 1, 1938, the price was cut to $0.6464+ again. (See Chart IV.) The domestic silver producer thus obtained a 33-cent (now 20-cent) per ounce subsidy for watering the national currency.

The proclamation of December 21, 1933, was followed by nothing very helpful to the silver interests for some months, except for the reaffirmation of the legal-tender quality of all coins, given in the Gold Reserve Act of 1934. In the Presidential message requesting that Act, the President had said that nothing further was to be done for silver until after more experience with the results of the December 21, 1933, proclamation.[9] True, there was a section in the Gold Reserve Act which permitted the President to devalue silver coins to the same degree by which he might devalue gold, but this provision was hardly necessary in view of the wide-open authority given him in the "Thomas" Amendment to coin silver in any ratio to gold.

SILVER PRESSURE

Immediately after the passage of the Gold Reserve Act of 1934, the inflationists and silverites renewed their pressure upon the Administration. The subterfuges, promises, and other hectic and furious activities that were engaged in, in order to strike while the inflation iron was still hot and while the temper of the nation was receptive to currency experiments, were numberless. The lengths to which the advocates of silver went in their alleged attempt to salvage the nation's currency and

---

[9] "I am, however, withholding any recommendation to the Congress looking to further extension of the monetary use of silver because I believe that we should gain more knowledge of the results of the London agreement and of our other monetary measures."

economy, but actually in a drive to aid their own speculators and producers, are a demonstration of the misinformation that can be foisted upon a nation by a small but powerful and determined pressure-group. The constant battering and hammering away by this group finally rammed a hole through the Administration's defenses. The extreme pressure caused first hesitation in the definite position taken by the Administration to do nothing more for silver, then retreat, and finally definite rout. The signal for complete capitulation was given by the silver message of the President on May 22, 1934.

The beginning of the silver campaign was seen in a proposed amendment to the Gold Reserve Act of 1934, which failed of adoption by only two votes. That proposal provided for large purchases of silver and the issuance of silver certificates against it. The varying fortunes of the silver drive throughout the first five months of 1934 were vividly reflected by silver prices which rose and fell "in speculative enthusiasm, as favorable or unfavorable interpretations were placed upon the progress of silver legislation in the United States; and plenty of opportunity was afforded for divergent views as it soon became evident after the convening of Congress that there existed considerable difference of opinion on the subject of silver between the Administration and the Legislature."[10]

Senator Wheeler's 16 to 1 measure was but one of many among the silver bills introduced by Pittman, Thomas, and many others. One bill, in an attempt to corral the silver and veterans' votes, proposed to buy silver and pay the soldiers' bonus with certificates. One of the bills which aimed to combine the farm vote with the silver vote was the Dies Bill. This bill provided that the Government was to buy American farm products, sell them abroad for silver bullion which would be valued at 10 to 25 percent more than the market value of the silver therein. Then the Government would pay the farmers with the silver. "The scheme combined the virtues of 'dumping' American goods on foreigners, taking vast quantities of silver off the world market, giving silver an artificial price, and inflating the currency with debased certificates. This monstros-

[10] Handy and Harman, *Annual Review*, 1934, pp. 7, 8.

ity passed the House by a large majority, and was reported out to the Senate."[11]

Various stages in the silver campaign are well summarized by Handy and Harman, in their *Annual Review*,[12] as follows:

Meanwhile the silver question was also being agitated in the House, and by March [1934] it was apparent that considerable strength had been mustered by the pro-silver group, which included not only representatives from the mining states but also agriculturalists and those favoring currency expansion. On March 10th the House Coinage Committee reported favorably on two measures, the Fiesinger Bill and the Dies Bill. In brief, the former called for Treasury purchases of domestic and foreign silver at the prevailing market in a total amount not to exceed 1,500,000,000 ounces; and the latter provided for the export of agricultural commodities against payment in silver, it being permissible to accept such silver at a price not in excess of 25 percent above market quotations. Presumably at the instigation of the Administration, Speaker Rainey forestalled action on the Fiesinger Bill, but on March 19th the House passed the Dies Bill by more than a two-thirds majority, its advocates claiming that this was a measure for the relief of domestic agriculture rather than monetary legislation. The following day [March 20] this [Dies] Bill was received by the Senate and referred to the Committee on Agriculture, which also had before it Senator Wheeler's proposal authorizing and directing the Government to purchase up to 1,500,000,000 ounces of silver for use as a reserve against note issues.

Recognizing the importance of concentrating their efforts on one measure, a sub-committee of the Senate Committee on Agriculture undertook the work of drafting amendments to the Dies Bill which would incorporate the ideas of the Senate silver bloc along the lines of the desired legislation. These amendments were favorably reported to the Senate on April 10th, and included provisions to nationalize domestic silver at the market price, and to buy silver abroad until either its price reached $1.29 per ounce or the 1926 price level for commodities was attained.

From this point, then, success was almost assured. Reports of conferences between the President and leaders of the silver bloc indicated that he was directing the course of silver legislation instead of waiting to "gain more knowledge of the results" of his previous silver measures. From being unalterably opposed to any but international means to rehabilitate silver, the President finally agreed to undertake domestic measures to provide that the monetary silver stock of the United States be increased.

Several other happenings in the early part of May stimulated the belief that the Administration was about to accede to the demands of the silverites. Rumored accumulations of silver by the Treasury, ambiguous statements by the Government, and definite statements by congressional leaders added more fuel to the speculative flame.[13]

THE SILVER PURCHASE ACT

Despite the opposition to silver legislation by monetary experts and economists and by both the conservative and liberal press, the Administration succumbed to the biased advice of certain interested senators, miners, and speculators. On May 22, 1934, the President issued his message on silver. That date was but four months and one week after his gold message, in which he had stated that he wished to "gain more knowledge of the results of the London Agreement and of our other monetary measures," before seeking any further action on silver. Excerpts from the Silver Message follow:

We should move forward as rapidly as conditions permit in broadening the metallic base of our monetary system and in stabilizing the purchasing and debt paying power of our money on a more equitable level . . . we should not neglect the value of an increased use of silver in improving our monetary system. Since 1929 that has been obvious.

Some measures for making a greater use of silver in the public interest are appropriate for independent action by us. On others international coöperation should be sought.

Of the former class is that of increasing the proportion of silver in the abundant metallic reserves back of our paper currency. This

[13] "During early May . . . the accumulation of substantial amounts of metal for spot and nearby New York delivery for an unknown account . . . was suspected to be the Treasury Department. Neither confirmation nor denial was forthcoming from Mr. Morgenthau at the time, but his later statement that the exchange stabilization fund had been used for this purpose, proved that the original suspicion had been correct. Further upward impetus was given to silver by statements from the White House and various Senators indicating that progress was being made in the formulation of legislation which met with the approval of both the President and the silver group." Handy and Harman, *Annual Review*, 1934, p. 11,

policy was initiated by the Proclamation of December 21, 1933 . . . We have since acquired other silver in the interest of stabilization of foreign exchange and the development of a broader metallic base for our currency. We seek to remedy a maladjustment of our currency.

The authority to purchase present accumulations of silver in this country should be limited to purchases at not in excess of 50 cents per ounce.

The Executive Authority should be enabled, should circumstances require, to take over present surpluses of silver in this country not required for industrial uses on payment of just compensation, and to regulate imports, exports and other dealings in monetary silver.

I, therefore, recommend legislation at the present session declaring it to be the policy of the United States to increase the amount of silver in our monetary stocks with the ultimate objective of having and maintaining one-fourth of their monetary value in silver and three-fourths in gold.

The Executive Authority should be authorized and directed to make the purchases of silver necessary to attain this ultimate objective.

While it is difficult to justify the message and the subsequent passage of the Silver Purchase Act, hindsight consideration of the economic conditions then extant, and analysis of practical politics, tend to soften one's appraisal of the situation. The inflationary fever of the nation, partly intensified it is true by the silverites, and the demand that the Government do something with money and take over its control from private hands, however unreasonable it was, did have to be granted some degree of satisfaction. The passage of the Silver Purchase Act, if it sated that demand, was hence not entirely unwarranted.

The Silver Purchase Act[14] was signed by the President on

---

[14] Following is a brief summary of the Act:
Purposes
   (1) To increase the price of silver
   (2) To increase the monetary stock of silver to one-third the value of the montetary gold stock
   (3) To issue silver certificates
Measures to be taken to achieve the purposes
   (1) Secretary of the Treasury to purchase silver at home and abroad upon terms and conditions he believes in the public interest
   (2) Purchases to cease when price reaches monetary value ($1.2929+ per fine ounce), or monetary silver stock equals one-third, in value, of monetary gold stock

June 19, 1934. It corresponded so closely with the Presidential message that one could almost be substituted for the other. The Act "declared it to be the policy of the United States that the proportion of silver to gold in the monetary stocks of the United States should be increased with the ultimate objective of having and maintaining one-fourth of the monetary value of such stocks in silver." Furthermore, "whenever the proportion of silver in the stocks of gold and silver is less than one-fourth, the Secretary of the Treasury is directed to purchase silver, at such times and upon such terms and conditions as he may deem reasonable and most advantageous to the public interest, but at a price not to exceed its monetary value and not to exceed 50 cents per fine ounce for silver situated in continental United States on May 1, 1934. He is required to issue silver certificates in face amount not less than the cost of all silver purchased under the act."[15] The monetary value here referred to, of course, is $1.2929+ per fine ounce.

The official summaries of the Act quote the Act as "directing" the Secretary of the Treasury to purchase silver. But he was *"authorized* and directed," and was given a large measure of discretion as to rates, terms, conditions, times of purchase, place, and so forth, "as he may deem reasonable and most advantageous to the public interest." [Italics mine.] This series of provisions is especially to be noted in light of the curt response later made to China, in answer to her protest at our Government's vigorous prosecution of the policy set forth in the Act.

Another section of the Act, which might just as well be forgotten for all the effect it will ever have, should be mentioned incidentally. It was stated that "whenever the market price of

---

(3) Price of silver situated in the United States on May 1, 1934, not to exceed $0.50 per fine ounce
(4) Silver to be sold when monetary silver stock exceeds one-third, in value, of monetary gold stock
(5) Silver certificates to be issued up to a face amount not less than the cost of the silver purchased
(6) Secretary of the Treasury may control import, export, and other transactions relating to silver
(7) President may "nationalize" silver
(8) Profit on purchase and sale of silver to be taxed 50 percent

[15] Secretary of the Treasury, *Annual Report,* 1934, p. 29.

silver exceeds its monetary value,[16] or the proportion of silver is greater than one-fourth of the monetary value of the total stocks of gold and silver, the Secretary of the Treasury may, with the approval of the President, sell any silver acquired under the Act; provided there is maintained a reserve in silver which, valued at its coinage price, shall not be less than the amount of silver certificates outstanding."[17]

The passage of the Act was a bonanza to the silver interests. But its influence was due to have widespread repercussions. It changed the "monetary reserve structure of this country and set in motion forces which shortly gave evidence of having far-reaching economic and political effects."[18]

One method by which the objective in the Act could have been realized within a minute or two of passage of the Act would have been for the President to revalue gold to $20.67 per ounce, and devalue silver coinage by an amount sufficient to bring its nominal monetary value to one-third that of gold. The President would have been entirely within the letter of the law, had he dared to do this. But, of course, that would have negated the real ends sought by the sponsors of the Act. Another method by which purchases of silver could be decreased would be to reduce the weight of the standard silver dollar. Had the President devalued the silver dollar to 59.06 percent of its present content, the amount of silver the Government would have needed to buy under the terms of the Silver Purchase Act would have been only about 250,000,000 ounces, instead of 1,329,000,000 ounces. However, the objective set up in the Act merely happened to be a convenient one to help the silver interests in their purposes, not one actually needed to improve upon the nation's currency and financial structure.

TAXING THE SILVER SPECULATOR

A sop thrown to the righteously indignant at the preferred treatment given speculators in silver, as well as other silver-market dealers, was the tax upon profits made from silver pur-

---

[16] See also *infra*, p. 61.
[17] Handy and Harman, *Annual Review*, 1934, p. 2.
[18] *Ibid.*, p. 1.

chases and sales from the time that final assurance of the Act's passage became apparent. The tax amounted to 50 percent of the net profit and was applicable to all transactions on or after May 15, 1934. Since the tax was aimed at the speculator, specific exemptions were made for legitimate business, that is, to persons whose regular business included the furnishing of silver for industrial, professional or artistic use; to industry; and to banks dealing in silver foreign exchange. Also exempted were certain transfers of silver bullion to the United States Government.

The Treasury undertook to curb the speculator in another manner. Under the Act the Secretary of the Treasury was authorized, with the approval of the President, "to regulate or prohibit the acquisition, importation, exportation, or transportation of silver and silver contracts." In view of the possibility of purchasing silver in the United States, shipping it abroad and waiting for the world price to rise,[19] as a result of United States policy, the Secretary of the Treasury issued an order on June 28, 1934, placing an embargo on the "exportation or transportation of silver from the continental United States except under license." Thereafter, it was possible for the New York market price to diverge somewhat from the London price, for a time at least.

"NATIONALIZATION" OF SILVER

In order to attain the alleged objective mentioned in the Act, two means were open to the Administration. One was to "nationalize" silver, the other was to purchase silver. First as to "nationalization." The President was "authorized at his discretion to require the delivery to the United States mints of any or all silver, in return for which shall be paid the monetary value of such silver in any form of United States coin or cur-

[19] "London quotations advanced further than the New York rates, with the result that it became profitable to buy silver in the United States and ship it abroad. Prompt recognition of this situation came on June 28th in the form of an order from Secretary Morgenthau placing an embargo, except under license, on all silver exports, which action prevented the outflow of metal into foreign hands and the necessity for its subsequent repurchase by the Government at prices which undoubtedly would have been higher." Handy and Harman, *Annual Review*, 1934, p. 13.

rency desired (less mint charges), provided that such value is not less than the market price of silver over a reasonable period previous to the date of the order."[20] He could, under the law, thus order any one in the United States to deliver all silver to the mints, at whatever price he saw fit, but at not more than $0.50 per fine ounce, and at an equitable value compared with the market price over a "reasonable" period of time. In return, currency was to be exchanged for such silver to the amount of its monetary value, less such deductions for seigniorage, brassage, coinage, and other mint charges as he should approve. Silver so acquired was to be coined into standard silver dollars or otherwise added to the monetary silver stocks of the United States.

On August 9, 1934, the President issued a proclamation and executive order which "required that all silver situated in the continental United States on August 9, 1934, with certain stipulated exemptions, be delivered to the United States mints within 90 days. The proclamation . . . directed the United States mints to receive for coinage or for addition to the monetary stocks of the United States any silver which the mint is satisfied was situated on August 9, 1934, in the continental United States, including the Territory of Alaska. For silver so received the United States mints were to return to the depositor an amount equal to 50.01 cents per fine troy ounce. The provisions of the proclamation were supplementary to the proclamation of December 21, 1933, with respect to the coinage of silver."[21]

The "certain stipulated exemptions" to which the order did not apply included silver held for industrial, professional, and artistic use, and silverware and fabricated articles; foreign and domestic coins; and newly mined domestic silver not subsequently processed to a fineness of over 0.8, which could be sold to the mints at $0.6464, under the President's proclamation of December 21, 1933. (See Chart IV.)

The price of $0.5001 per fine ounce was just over the $0.50 stipulated in the law, but it was held that that price was set for

[20] Secretary of the Treasury, *Annual Report,* 1934, p. 29.
[21] *Ibid.,* 1935, p. 41.

convenience in the mint calculations of seigniorage, etc. The deduction from the monetary value amounted to 61 8/25 percent.

While the Administration lost little time in its steps toward "nationalization," it waited long enough to have to pay $0.5001 per ounce, instead of $0.45 to $0.45125 per ounce, which is all it would have paid if it had nationalized within a day or two of the passage of the Act. The total amount of silver national-

Chart V

SILVER ACQUISITION BY THE UNITED STATES TREASURY, SINCE DECEMBER, 1933

(Chart Shows Cumulated Acquisitions since Inception of the Program)

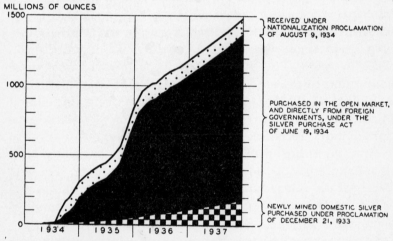

Source: United States Treasury Department.

ized at the $0.50 price, was 113,028,500 ounces, costing $56,-525,553. (See Charts V and VI.) At $0.45125 per ounce, this would have cost $51,004,111, thus saving the Government $5,521,442. But $5,521,442 is small in comparison with the $89,608,995 seigniorage "profit" made by the Government on the nationalized silver.

Now, instead of being only two commodities, silver became three commodities. There was, first, open-market silver, which came into the United States after August 9, 1934, and to which the open-market price applied. Then, secondly, there was the newly mined domestic silver, which had been in a special class since December 21, 1933, and for which the Government paid $0.6464 per fine ounce, until, in April, 1935, the price was raised twice, first to $0.7111 and then to $0.7757.[22] The third

Chart VI

SOURCES OF SILVER ACQUISITIONS BY THE UNITED STATES TREASURY

(December 21, 1933, to December 31, 1937)

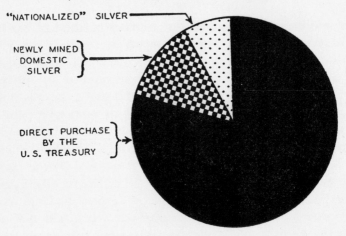

TABLE OF ACQUISITIONS

	Millions of Fine Ounces	Percent
"Nationalized" Silver (Proclamation of August 9, 1934)	113	7.6
Newly Mined Domestic Silver (Proclamation of December 21, 1933)	192	12.9
Direct Purchase Silver (Silver Purchase Act of June 19, 1934)	1,180	79.5
Total	1,485	100.0

Source: United States Treasury Department.

class consisted of silver situated in the United States on August 9, 1934, for which the Government paid $0.5001 per fine ounce. (See Chart IV.) Thus one commodity became three commodities, and each of the three, hence, had its own distinct price. The absurdity of the situation is well illustrated by the follow-

[22] But reduced on January 1, 1938, to $0.6464, again.

ing quotation. "The delivery of the proper silver caused many complications, particularly in the case of industry, where factory supplies had to be maintained pending foreign importations, and where identification became impossible due to processing of the material."[23] "However," this publication goes on to say, "due to the Government's desire to restrict legitimate enterprise as little as possible in carrying out its monetary policy, a solution to these problems was found with the co-operation of the trade."

PURCHASE OF SILVER

In addition to nationalization, another method of reaching the objective was made available to the Secretary of the Treasury—that of direct purchase. The Secretary was authorized to buy and sell silver at home and abroad, and at any price he deemed to be in the public interest. However, he was not to buy when the price of silver exceeded its monetary value, or $1.2929+ per fine ounce; nor, obviously, was he to buy when the one-to-three objective had been attained. The limitation on purchase after the monetary value was reached by the market price was of course to prove ineffective. During the present century the market value of silver has approached the monetary value only in the unusual post-war years, and that only when the Treasury was replenishing its stock subsequent to the Pittman Act. Before that, the latest date at which silver had been anywhere near even $1.00 an ounce was in 1890 and 1891, again a period of United States Treasury purchasing. It thus seems that the mystic monetary value of $1.2929+ per fine ounce is but a hang-over from a period long before the Civil War, when silver was still being considered not merely as a commodity but as a basic money by a substantial portion of the commercial and industrial world.

As to the second ground for ceasing the purchase of silver, that the one-to-three objective had been reached, there was little belief at the time that it would in any way serve as a bar. First, it was thought very unlikely that China would allow any of her silver to go out of the nation. Secondly, the world's new production which could be diverted to United States monetary

[23] Handy and Harman, *Annual Review,* 1934, pp. 16, 17.

use was estimated at from 120,000,000 to 200,000,000 ounces per year.[24] In order to obtain enough silver from new production to reach the one-to-three objective, which at that time required the purchase of 1,329,000,000 ounces more than was then held in the United States monetary stock, this Government would have had to purchase all that new silver for the next seven to twelve years.

The first premise broke down, with woeful results for the silverites in the United States. While China officially barred the export of silver, it was almost impossible to prevent smuggling from China, or to prevent the Japanese-aided export through the northern provinces. From the very beginning of operations under the Silver Purchase Act, China began to feel the pinch.[25] The dumping of China's supply into the United States was of little help to domestic producers, however much it helped the silver speculators. Also, the adverse effects upon China's economy helped no one.[26]

The vigor with which the Treasury pushed the silver program, plus this wholesale dumping by the Far East, worked to bring nearer the time when the one-to-three ratio of silver to gold would be reached. But all such calculations went awry because of what happened to gold, rather than as regards silver. The phenomenal increase in the United States gold stock, due in some part to increased domestic production but in much larger part to imports, kept pushing the attainment of the silver objective farther and farther away. The more silver the Treasury acquired, the more it had to acquire, in order even to keep up with the increase in the gold stock, let alone approach the ratio.

When the Silver Purchase Act was passed, silver stocks were

[24] Handy and Harman, *Annual Review*, 1934, p. 6.

[25] "China, however, was an even larger source of supply than newly mined metal, which fact is most interesting when we recall that as recently as 1930 that country absorbed nearly 125,000,000 ounces in one year. We are advised that during the first eleven months of 1934 Chinese net exports of silver bullion and specie amounted to 185,000,000 ounces, and we estimate a total of 200,000,-000 ounces for the full year, which includes an allowance for the smuggling that assumed sizable proportions in the last quarter." Handy and Harman, *Annual Review*, 1934, p. 29.

[26] See later sections for an account of China's financial misfortunes which stemmed from American silver policy.

valued at one-ninth of gold stocks. One year later, despite vigorous prosecution of the policy,[27] the ratio was still under one-sixth, as compared with the ratio of one-third which was sought. Two years after passage of the Act, silver stocks had reached just over 21 percent of the gold stocks, and have remained there ever since. After draining the world of much of its needed silver, it is difficult to see how the Treasury can purchase much more. United States silver stocks have been almost trebled, from $900,000,000 in June, 1934, to more than $2,700,000,000 at present, but gold stocks, over the same period, have risen from less than $8,000,000,000 to almost $13,000,000,000. The ratio between the stocks of the two metals in the United States has just about reached the levels obtaining prior to devaluation of the gold dollar. (See Chart VII.)

EFFECT ON CHINA

The literal interpretation placed upon the mandate in the Silver Purchase Act by the Treasury resulted in great hardship in silver-using nations. Within two months after the passage of the Act, China began to feel the pinch of being deprived of her basic money.[28] The increased price of silver led to its outflow, and consequently set in motion a deflation process for China. This meant lower prices and tighter money. Also, because of such currency appreciation, there was a tendency, temporarily

[27] "It is estimated that the total [amount of silver] acquired [during the year following the passage of the Act] was 12 times as much silver as was produced in the United States in the same period, 17.5 times as much of that production as was available for monetary use, 2.2 times the total world production, and 2.9 times the current world output available for monetary use." Secretary of the Treasury, *Annual Report*, 1935, p. 42.

[28] "China began to feel the adverse effects of our policy soon after the Silver Purchase Act was passed. For precisely the same reasons that devaluation of the dollar here was considered a measure of recovery, the cheapening of silver in the depression years had brought a boom to China.

"Since silver was the money of China, a decline in its value meant not merely a rise in domestic Chinese prices but it also meant that China had acquired a trade advantage similar to that obtained by Western nations through currency depreciation.

"When the price of silver began to rise in London in response to our purchases, silver began to flow out of China. People took paper currency to the banks and obtained silver for it; then sent the silver to London to sell to our Treasury. Soon money became scarce in China, credit became dear, prices fell, business and banks failed and trade stagnated." E. V. Bell, "Silver Law Reaches Its Climax in China," in the New York *Times* of November 10, 1935.

at least, to an adverse foreign-trade balance. As stated prophetically by Professor Sprague, "A decidedly higher price for silver than now obtains would be unwelcome in China, just as it would be unwelcome in most of the countries now on a paper basis to return to gold as the basis of a very considerable appreciation of their currency."[29]

Chart VII

MONETARY SILVER STOCK OF THE UNITED STATES, AND ITS RATIO TO THE MONETARY GOLD STOCK

(As of the End of Each Month)

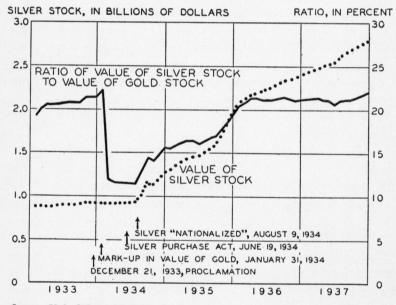

Source: United States Treasury Department.

China communicated with Washington in an attempt to secure some relief from the financial hardships she saw approaching. She sought a modification of the silver-purchase program of the United States Treasury, because of the harmful effects on her domestic economy. For in view of the fact that China was on a silver standard, she had to permit the unrestricted

[29] O. M. W. Sprague, *Recovery and Common Sense,* p. 90.

movement of silver. Consequently, heavy losses of silver took place in the first nine months of 1934, partly to offset her adverse trade balance, and partly to speculate on increasing silver prices. The loss of China's monetary silver stock naturally affected her bank reserves and resulted in falling prices and monetary deflation. The situation is likened to that which existed in the United States during the first two months of 1933. In this connection it might be well to recall the pleas of the silver interests, in 1932 and 1933, when it was urged that the price of silver be increased in order to restore purchasing power to half the world's population.

Although individual bankers in China had raised objections to the silver price-raising policy as early as February, 1934, the Government did not do so until August. Again in September, and also in October, the Chinese Government protested to the United States Government. The Chinese Government had suggested, also, that one way to offset her difficulties would be to exchange some of her silver for gold, directly with the United States Treasury.

After making only evasive replies, the United States Government, finally, on October 12, 1934, gave answer to China that the Administration was merely carrying out the policy enunciated and expressly directed by Congress. In Secretary Hull's reply, he stated that the policy was statutory and mandatory upon the Treasury Department as to its general objective. He stated, too, that full consideration would be accorded China's contention. As for the direct exchange of silver for gold, he indicated that there was no such need because of the existence of free gold and silver markets in which any nation could make purchases and sales.[30]

Although the law did enunciate general policy as to silver purchases, it also gave the Secretary of the Treasury discretionary power as to time and place of such purchase, terms, conditions, and so forth. As will be shown later, the Secretary did not hesitate to use his discretion, in the following and succeeding years, when it suited his purposes.

[30] But see *infra*, pp. 71 n., 74, 129.

CHINA ABANDONS THE SILVER STANDARD

When China saw in Secretary Hull's cable of October 12, 1934, the uselessness of attempting to sway a stubborn Administration, she imposed an export levy on silver and thus, *de facto,* left the silver standard. Smuggling developed and China continued to lose silver. Finally, on November 3, 1935, China abandoned the silver standard *de jure.*

Official announcement was made on October 15, 1934, that henceforth the export duty upon silver was to be increased to 10 percent and, in addition, an equalization charge, which was to vary with the world price of silver, was to be superimposed upon it.[31]

Although the tax and embargo were expected to put a halt to the loss of silver by China, they were of little avail. True, the direct and legitimate shipment of silver from China to the United States was stopped by these actions, but the drain continued. Because of the subsequent depreciation of the yuan, the profit to be made by smuggling silver out of China was very large. Smuggling, therefore, did develop, largely through North China and Japan, and it has even been claimed that during 1935 the amount of Chinese silver to reach London through various channels "was comparable in volume to the supplies" from China in 1934. Shanghai silver stocks, which were estimated at close to 450,000,000 ounces in June, 1934, had fallen to around 250,000,000 ounces by the end of 1934. This level continued unchanged until October, 1935, when the figures were no longer reported.

By the autumn of 1935, there were recurrent rumors of China's abandonment of the silver standard. Finally, on November 3, 1935, the Chinese Government announced a new

---

[31] The customs duties on exports of silver were fixed as follows:

"On silver dollars and mint bars, 10% less 2¼% minting charges paid, i.e., 7¾% net.

"On other forms of silver, 10% (in lieu of 2¼% previously charged).

"In addition, an equalization charge will be imposed upon exports of silver equal to the deficiency, if any, existing between the theoretical parity of London silver and the rate of exchange officially fixed by the Central Bank of China, after making allowance for the export duty.

"This tax, which could be increased or decreased daily by means of the equalization fee, was expected to curtail materially the flow of silver from China, which was a bullish factor." Handy and Harman, *Annual Review,* 1934, pp. 18, 19.

monetary policy, which definitely removed her from the silver standard. The series of decrees, effective November 4, 1935, provided for the compulsory delivery of all silver coin and bullion to the Government, and for the issue of an inconvertible paper currency to be managed with the object of maintaining a stable value for the yuan in terms of foreign currencies. The main features of these decrees are as follows:

(1) "Nationalization" of silver; holders of silver to exchange it for bank notes

(2) Note issue to be restricted to the three Government-controlled banks only

(3) Chinese dollar to be pegged at the then existing level by foreign-exchange operations of the three banks

(4) Central Bank of China to be reorganized as a reserve bank

China thus *de jure* confirmed what she had done *de facto* in October, 1934. By the levying of restrictions and flexible charges at that time, China had actually abandoned silver for a managed currency. Even though silver continued to be used as bank reserves and currency, its price no longer determined the value of the Chinese dollar in foreign exchange.

China's abandonment of silver lost to the silver producers one of their most steady and substantial markets. Ironically, the very policy which was adopted in order "to do something for silver" boomeranged right back, and dealt the industry one of its greatest blows since the commercial world abandoned silver as part of their monetary standard in favor of gold. As one writer has said, China, "the last country on earth with a silver standard, had been forced to drop it. The silver bloc had killed the silver goose."[32]

One authority,[33] at least, questions whether China should remain off silver permanently. Abstracts from its *Reviews* follow:

China has been forced to abandon the silver standard in order to protect herself against depletion of bank reserves and a price deflation. Although it is too soon to predict whether this program can be carried out with complete success, nevertheless, we can foresee that considerable difficulty may be encountered by the Nanking

[32] Carothers, *Silver in America*, p. 31.
[33] Handy and Harman, *Annual Review*, 1935, p. 50; 1936, pp. 9–14, 30.

Government in making effective the nationalization of silver. It would seem preferable for China to return to the silver standard, with silver at a price which would represent a satisfactory exchange level for her internal economy. Such a solution would undoubtedly prove agreeable to Hongkong as well.

China has now been on a managed foreign exchange standard for over a year and the new system has worked well, although it is difficult to venture a positive opinion at the present time as to how completely exchange has been divorced from the price of silver. This much, however, may be said—that if the price should score a substantial rise, its effect upon Chinese currency would be nil, although it is probable that surplus silver in China would be sold both by the Government and by smugglers. On the other hand, if the silver market should take a severe drop, the public might become nervous regarding the adequacy of the reserve and jump to the conclusion, however unwarranted, that the Chinese dollar might be further devalued.

Under the present currency system of China, silver is no longer necessary as a reserve, although the Government has agreed to maintain in silver a sufficient proportion of the total reserves to equal in value at least 25 percent of the note issue. Nor is silver necessary as a circulating medium for payments within the country. We are told that the public in China has acquired so much confidence in the legal tender notes of the Government banks that they are no longer metallic-minded. If the proposed new token silver coins should be minted, which has not been done as yet, the public will be fully prepared to accept them, not as silver coins but as coins whose value is largely fiduciary. As to the old silver coins which have so far not been surrendered to the Government since the nationalization order was proclaimed, their circulation is impossible because they cannot now be freely transferred either by individuals or through the agency of banks. According to advices from Shanghai, the chances of silver again becoming the Chinese monetary standard are very remote, and will depend upon what arrangements the United States may desire to make with China. As the possibility of competitive devaluation of world currencies is not yet entirely removed, it is inconceivable that China will again commit herself to a silver standard without some definite understanding with the United States, which is the only other important country still using silver as a part of its reserve.

It remains to be seen whether China, long accustomed to the use of metallic money, can permanently function on a managed exchange basis, but the success of the experiment so far is well presented by Dr. H. H. Kung, Chinese Minister of Finance, in an article published in the China Press, from which we quote:

"The new currency policy has been operating smoothly and facts bear out its gratifying results. . . Since the enforcement of the currency decree of November 3rd, 1935, exchange stability has been maintained at a degree never before experienced in China, and the resources available therefore have been considerably increased. . . Also, external currency reserves have been substantially augmented as the result of sales of large amounts of silver to the American Government, 50,000,000 ounces having been negotiated in November, 1935, and further sizable amounts negotiated in May, 1936. The resulting credit in foreign currency has materially contributed to the successful stabilization of China's currency. In May, 1936, the Government announced that it will continue its policy to maintain adequate reserves against note issue consisting of gold, foreign exchange, and silver, the silver portion of the reserves to have a value equivalent to at least 25 percent of the note circulation. . . For the first time in history, China has succeeded in adopting a fundamentally modern and truly national monetary policy. Its adoption was a veritable revolution in China's monetary system, even though in this the Chinese Government was only following the example of most other nations in recent years. . . The new currency policy is in accordance with the trend of the present-day economic world, and promises a better day for those nations which trade and coöperate with China, as well as for China herself."

In China, although a managed foreign exchange standard has proved satisfactory during the past year, the new system has not yet been put to a real test. At some future date, the Chinese Government may consider it advisable to increase the use of silver for reserve or monetary purposes, or even to make a partial return to the silver standard; but certainly they would hesitate to take such a step, without assurance that the safety of their financial structure would not again be jeopardized by some subsequent action of the United States.

UNITED STATES TREASURY THE PRINCIPAL SILVER BUYER

Now to resume discussion of the operations of the United States Treasury after the "nationalization" decree of August 9, 1934. Except for continuation of its purchases, thus forcing silver prices upward, little of significance occurred until the spring of 1935. The Treasury had become the principal buyer in the market, and in fact was the only buyer except for the small amounts taken by industry and the arts. The silver market of the New York Commodity Exchange had closed in August, 1934, thus eliminating the public as a factor in the market.

Silver of foreign origin, which was refined in the United States, was not eligible for sale to the Government at the price of the newly mined domestic silver, nor could it be exported, because of Treasury decrees. Hence the Government was forced to support the New York price.

This situation became especially pronounced in January, 1935, when heavy selling resulted from a misinterpretation of a statement in President Roosevelt's budget message in connection with silver seigniorage profits. It was thought that the President indicated curtailment of the silver-buying program. Hence, on the day that the budget was made public, January 8, the Treasury had to be an especially heavy buyer in the New York market.

On April 26, 1935, world prices reached a peak of $0.81. This advance resulted from demands by manufacturers who were attempting to protect themselves against what seemed to be a runaway market. In the meantime the United States Government had twice increased its purchase price for newly mined domestic silver. First, on April 10, it raised the price from $0.6464+ to $0.7111 per fine ounce, and again on April 24, it raised the price to $0.7757. When, on April 27, it was seen that the Treasury would not continue to raise the domestic price, fears arose that the advance had been going along too fast, and on that one day prices fell by $0.0425.

SILVER COINS TO THE MELTING POT

The high price offered by the United States Government for both foreign and domestic silver threatened the silver of the whole world. Because the Treasury was doing much of its buying in the New York market, that market began to import foreign silver coins, in order to melt them down and sell the silver content.

Accordingly, on May 20, 1935, the Secretary of the Treasury, with the approval of the President, issued an order prohibiting the import into the United States of "foreign silver coins and other conventional pieces or forms of silver commonly used in any foreign country as money or coin" whose monetary value was less than 110 percent of the open-market value of its silver bullion content. This of course was only a stopgap, and as a saving feature was practically without effect.

In addition to China, all other nations which used silver to any large extent also suffered from the disturbances to which our silver policy gave rise.[34] As early as January, 1935, Mexico became restive. The temporary assuagement of her irritation at that time was offset towards the end of April when, because of the rise of silver prices, the bullion value of the peso was above its monetary value. Hence, in order to prevent the peso from being shipped to the United States either as a coin or in melted-down form, President Cardenas proclaimed a bank holiday on April 27. Then he ordered all coins to be exchanged for paper currency, and prohibited the export of silver money. At the time it was thought that silver would no longer circulate in Mexico. But a year and a half later, when silver prices had fallen, these orders were revoked and silver coinage was restored. On September 1, 1936, the Mexican Government restored silver money to its former fineness of 72 percent. This repealed the monetary decree of April 27, 1935, which had ordered the exchange of the silver then in circulation for a paper one-peso note and a half-peso silver coin of 42 percent fineness. But in that year and a half interval, Mexico, by debasing her silver coinage, had had to "take action contrary to the spirit" of the London silver agreement.

China and Mexico, however, were not the only nations to feel the detrimental repercussions of the American silver pol-

[34] "Meanwhile, the situation has become entangled with international politics. In January [1935] Mexico's indignation over the disturbance of her currency was assuaged at a dinner of Mexican officials, Treasury officials and silver Senators in Washington. Apparently the *amende* offered was an understanding, not made public, as to our purchases of Mexican silver and our price policy. It developed also that at the time of the Chinese crisis in 1935 another non-public arrangement was made with China, as a result of which we paid her 65 cents an ounce for silver worth 45 cents. As this is written word comes of a new agreement under which, apparently, China is obliged to retain at least 25 percent of her future metallic reserves in silver and to circulate debased silver coins. In return we are to buy large amounts of her silver and pay for it in gold.

"China is apparently to have a sort of managed currency with mixed gold and silver reserves. Unless she returns to a new and devalued silver standard she must some time determine whether to tie her currency to an English, Japanese or American base. Sterling is the logical choice, but Japan has already expressed angry threats in regard to this. 'Doing something for silver' to help the Chinese has had some unexpected consequences." Carothers, *Silver in America*, p. 33.

icy. Not only did Mexico have to demonetize her silver coinage and undertake a managed currency, but nations all over the world were hurt by the rise. Most of the protective measures they were forced to take for their silver coinage reduced the use of silver.

The silver coinage debasement campaign to keep coins from the melting pot was world-wide. Central America, South America, Europe, Asia and even Africa participated.

On April 3rd [1935], Costa Rica forbade the export of silver coins and bars; and in August a new base metal currency was authorized. On May 3rd, Peru prohibited the purchase, sale, hoarding, and exportation of silver coins; and the exportation of silver in other forms, except newly mined material. A subsequent decree authorized a new subsidiary coinage of copper and nickel, which was to be minted in London. By May 17th, Guatemala, Ecuador, and Colombia had followed suit with embargoes upon silver exports; and in July, the legislature of the latter country authorized the withdrawal of silver coins from circulation.

In Europe, we find that the Free City of Danzig decreed the withdrawal of the only silver coins in circulation, the 5 and 2 gulden pieces; and approved the sale of the resultant bullion. The Bank of Spain prepared for higher silver prices by printing a large supply of 5 and 10 peseta notes, which were held in readiness for issue should the silver peseta begin to disappear from circulation. Italy's decree, withdrawing silver money and prohibiting hoarding, was primarily a war measure; but her opponent, Ethiopia, was obliged to ban the export of currency because smuggling of the thaler had already commenced.

Traveling further eastward, we learn that silver coins in some of the frontier cities of Persia commanded a premium over their face value, and that the Government at Teheran had authorized an issue of subsidiary copper coins to replace the silver currency lost through smuggling. The Siamese Government was reported to be awaiting a favorable opportunity to dispose of the silver content of the coin reserve, equivalent to nearly 1,000,000 ounces, because of the fact that the silver baht could not be made to circulate. Advices from Singapore stated that, during the period of peak silver prices, the Straits Settlement Treasury issued a number of worn 5 cent pieces of the 1917–18 issue, which contained less silver than the present currency. This measure was only temporary because of the later decline in the market, but during the emergency it served to prevent hoarding and melting of the coinage.

Effective at noon on November 9th, the Government of the Crown Colony of Hongkong prohibited the export of Hongkong dollars and silver subsidiary coins, Mexican dollars, and silver bullion; thus supplementing the embargo which existed on the shipment of Chinese silver coin except to China. This action was preliminary to the adoption of a managed currency, which became effective on December 5th through an ordinance of the Legislative Council ordering the withdrawal of silver from circulation; amending the legal tender laws; and establishing a fund to stabilize exchange. On account of the close commercial relationship between Hongkong and China, such action was necessary in order to bring Hongkong exchange back to the parity with China's currency which had existed formerly.[35]

The story of the debasement of silver coins, the abandonment of the silver standard, and financial chaos in China contrasts strangely with some portions of President Roosevelt's Silver Message of May 22, 1934.

Some measures for making a greater use of silver in the public interest are appropriate for independent action by us. On others, international coöperation should be sought. . . Concerted action by all nations, or at least a large group of nations, is necessary if a permanent measure of value, including both gold and silver, is eventually to be made a world standard. . . At no time since the efforts of this nation to secure international agreement on silver began in 1878 have conditions been more favorable for making progress along this line. Accordingly, I have begun to confer with some of our neighbors in regard to the use of both silver and gold, preferably on a coördinated basis, as a standard of monetary value. Such an agreement would constitute an important step forward toward a monetary unit of value more equitable and stable in its purchasing and debt paying power.

THE FALL IN SILVER PRICES

Silver prices began to toboggan in May, 1935. But the first real sign of weakness in the situation appeared during the last week of June. The London market was swamped by heavy selling orders from the Indian bazaars at the time of their June settlement, and by increased Chinese offerings. The United States Treasury continued to purchase large amounts of spot silver, but its bids were at successively lower rates. By July,

[35] Handy and Harman, *Annual Review*, 1935, pp. 17, 18, 40-42.

prices were receding so rapidly that during that month and the succeeding one the Treasury had to buy silver very heavily in world markets in an endeavor to prevent a complete collapse of silver prices. The Secretary of the Treasury announced that more than twenty-five million ounces had been bought on August 14, 1935. But the effect on prices was practically nil. The New York price, which had averaged 74 cents in May, fell to as low as 49¾ cents on December 24, and averaged 58 cents in that month. A further decline to 45 cents in the next two months brought silver prices to the level at which they have subsequently remained for more than two years. (See Chart IV.)

The really violent slide suffered by silver occurred in the last two months of 1935. Beginning late in October and lasting through the first week in December, demoralization was so bad in the London market that there were no quotations for either spot or futures, but only a discount on forward delivery.

The American Treasury, which had been the chief purchaser in the silver market throughout the year, announced on December 19, 1935, that United States purchases consisted mainly of newly mined silver of Mexico and Peru. In the following year, Canada and some additional South American countries were added to the list of nations from which the Treasury made direct purchases. In that year, the Chinese Government also was included.

Also, by 1936, the United States Treasury began to let up on its silver purchases. From a monthly high of 92,000,000 ounces purchased in each of the months of October and November, 1935, the takings fell to between ten and twenty million ounces a month. Open-market prices of course reflected the easing of the pressure. Prices averaged just over 47 cents in January, and went as low as 44.8 cents (monthly average) during the five months beginning with June.[36]

---

[36] "The year 1936 has been an exceptionally quiet and uneventful one for silver, a condition reflected by unusually narrow market fluctuations. In fact, there has been only one other year since the turn of the century in which the New York price showed less of a spread between the high and low points. In 1909 the range was 3⅞¢, which compares with a 5¢ figure for the past twelve months, and a variation of only 2¾¢ if the first three weeks of January are eliminated." Handy and Harman, *Annual Review*, 1936, p. 1.

If the pre-gold-devaluation price of silver of 25 cents be multiplied by 1.69,[37] the result would be 42½ cents, which is but slightly under current market prices. This seems to bear out a statement made in 1933 that the only way to secure a substantial rise in the world price of silver is in the resumption of large importations of the metal by India and China, rather than in the monetary tinkering by the United States Government.[38]

The return of silver prices to their former levels, after allowance for the devaluation of the gold dollar, thus indicates one thing. That is that permanent price-fixing is practically impossible for silver as for other commodities, however powerful the agency which attempts it and however widespread the operations it undertakes.

SILVER CERTIFICATES

The issue of silver certificates based upon silver acquired by the United States was started with the very first of such silver acquisitions—the war-debt receipts under the "Thomas" Amendment of May 12, 1933. The issuance of these silver certificates against the silver accepted from foreign governments in payment of indebtedness to the United States was begun on January 13, 1934.[39] The certificates were required to be issued up to the value at which the silver was received from the for-

[37] The reciprocal of 59.06 percent, the level to which the gold dollar was devalued.

[38] "In our opinion, the paramount factor affecting silver during the past year was the tremendous shrinkage in demand from the Orient. Ordinarily India and China absorb approximately 75% of the world production of newly mined metal. In 1929 when production reached its peak of 260,900,000 ounces, the net imports of these two countries amounted to 218,500,000 ounces, or nearly 84%. Similar percentages for 1930 and 1931 were 88% and 60%. During the past year, although production declined to 160,600,000 ounces, India and China consumed only 52,000,000 ounces, or 32%.

". . . Eliminating from consideration the enhancement of silver by means of re-monetization, it is our conviction that an economically sound higher level for the white metal is contingent *solely* upon an increased demand for it from the Far East; and such demand can arise only when India and China can sell their products in greater volume and at higher prices in the world markets. A revival of trade and higher levels for commodities, therefore, would appear to be essential for the betterment of silver." Handy and Harman, *Annual Review*, 1932, pp. 20, 21. [Italics mine.]

[39] Secretary of the Treasury, *Annual Report*, 1934, p. 29.

eign Governments; a later law permitted the issue of certificates up to the full monetary value of that silver.[40]

The Silver Purchase Act authorized and directed the Secretary of the Treasury to issue silver certificates equal to the cost of all the silver purchased, and to place them in circulation. In a letter to the author, the Treasury Department stated that sil-

[40] "The Gold Reserve Act of 1934 authorized the President to issue silver certificates against 'any silver bullion, silver, or standard silver dollars in the Treasury not then held for the redemption of any outstanding certificates.' Under this act, silver certificates became issuable against any unencumbered silver in the Treasury, irrespective of the authority under which the silver was received.

"It was decided, therefore, to provide a single or consolidated series of silver certificates for issuance against any free silver held in the Treasury. Consequently payment of the certificates specifically prepared for issuance against silver received from foreign governments under the act of May 12, 1933, was discontinued, and issues of certificates under that and later authorizations awaited the preparation of the consolidated series.

"This consolidated series of new silver certificates has been given the designation, 'Series of 1934.'" Secretary of the Treasury, *Annual Report*, 1934, p. 30.

"In a series of orders (summarized in the letter of the Secretary of the Treasury to the President, September 10, 1934, approved by the President September 12, 1934, and supplemented by the letters of the Under Secretary of the Treasury to the Treasurer, March 1 and April 5, 1935), the issuance and maintenance as part of the money circulation of the United States of silver certificates were authorized and directed in a face amount equal to the total of the following items:

" (a) The amount of silver dollars held by the Treasury.

" (b) $80,000,000, being an amount approximately equal to the monetary value of all of the silver bullion in the Treasury on June 14, 1934, not then held for redemption of any outstanding silver certificates. This amount does not include silver held in the stabilization fund on June 14, 1934.

" (c) $1,560,000, being the amount of silver certificates of the series of 1933 outstanding on March 12, 1934 (including those held in the Treasurer's cash). Silver certificates of the series of 1934 will be issued in lieu of silver certificates of the series of 1933 as they are redeemed or otherwise received into the Treasury and retired.

" (d) A sum equal to the amount heretofore or hereafter returned to the depositors for silver received at the United States mints and assay offices on and after June 15, 1934, whether under the proclamation of December 21, 1933 (relating to newly-mined domestic silver), or under the proclamation of August 9, 1934 (relating to the nationalization of silver stocks).

" (e) A sum equal to the cost of all silver heretofore or hereafter purchased under the authority of section 3 of the Silver Purchase Act of 1934, whether purchased from the stabilization fund or from other sources.

"Since there was a considerable reserve stock of silver certificates of the series of 1928, the Treasurer was directed to issue them until the stock was exhausted. The last of these certificates was issued on July 6, 1935. On June 30, 1935, the amount of silver certificates outstanding was $810,040,419, representing an increase of $315,044,005 during the fiscal year." Secretary of the Treasury, *Annual Report*, 1935, p. 43.

ver certificates are currently being issued only up to the cost value of the silver, and that the difference between the cost price of the silver and its monetary value is entered in the Treasury Statements as "seigniorage."

"ACCOMPLISHMENTS" OF THE SILVER POLICY

Just what did the United States silver policy accomplish? Were its results largely in the monetary field, in international affairs or in a bounty to a comparatively insignificant domestic industry? The question can be considered with respect to the effect on silver prices, on silver production, on other nations, and on general monetary conditions within this country.

Did our policy raise silver prices? As pointed out above, the open-market prices of silver have not been permanently changed. Approximately the same amount of silver exchanges for a specific amount of gold now as four years ago. In terms of a depreciated currency, of course, the price is higher. It is true that the domestic producer gets a bounty which until recently amounted to about 33 cents above the open-market price of 45 cents. But that bounty could have been given him in the first place, without the necessity of going through the pseudo-monetary and detrimental international operations in which this nation has taken part. From the price point of view, therefore, one can not escape the conclusion that this Government's silver policy consisted of unnecessary, dangerous, and wasted actions. A direct grant of the bounty would have been more economical as well as more effective, and much more desirable from the monetary and international viewpoints discussed below.

Silver production in the United States has increased very sharply since the lows of 1933. (See Chart VIII.) Indeed, 1937 production is estimated to be almost three times the 1933 output. Part of the increase was undoubtedly due to the Government price subsidy, and part to the general industrial recovery. The latter factor is especially significant where silver is chiefly a by-product of the production of other industrial metals.[41] In

---

[41] About two-thirds of silver production is by-product of copper and lead output.

these industries the by-product silver would have been produced anyhow. As to the producers primarily of silver, their output could have been stimulated by a subsidy without the attendant silver-policy operations undertaken by the Government.

The improvement which was anticipated in American foreign trade also failed to materialize. Trade with China de-

Chart VIII

SILVER PRODUCTION IN THE UNITED STATES

(Monthly)

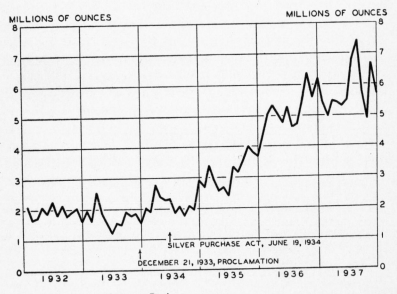

Source: *Survey of Current Business.*

clined, and the consequent loss of goodwill may postpone reëstablishment of that trade for an extended period. Indeed, some of those who advocated higher prices for silver as an aid to China now suggest that such higher prices prevent the importations of goods made by Chinese coolie labor.

Thus the international field shows no results from the pursuit of our silver policies except those which have been harmful to others as well as to ourselves.[42]

Finally, the effects of the silver policies on the monetary structure of this country are noteworthy. Their magnitude is illustrated by the increase in our silver stocks from only $900,-000,000 in early 1934 to $2,800,000,000 by the end of 1937. This means that bullion worth at market between $870,000,000 and $980,000,000 is backing almost three billion dollars' worth of currency. Thus the currency has been watered, on silver account, by almost two billion dollars.

Perhaps such watering was useful and necessary. Senator Pittman in a speech at New York[43] said a metallic base was needed for currency issues, and that since there was not enough gold to serve as a base, silver was needed. He also mentioned the maldistribution of gold, but, to this author at least, this maldistribution points to the opposite conclusion. The Senator attempted to rationalize his stand by pointing out that silver was not new to our currency system but was a main part of it until 1873, and that even in 1900 over 30 percent of our currency was silver.

He advanced two other arguments which were strongly contradicted by later events. He said that the silver bills then in

[42] "If one desires a record of complete failure to bring about international cooperation in the wider use of silver as a monetary metal, it is only necessary to review the happenings of the past year. Demonetization of silver coinage occurred, or was threatened, throughout the world; and China and Hongkong, the only important adherents to the silver standard, abandoned that standard in favor of managed currencies." Handy and Harman, *Annual Review*, 1935, pp. 44, 45.

"In our last year's 'Review' we pointed out that the Silver Purchase Act had, up to that time, failed to accomplish the purposes for which this piece of legislation was intended; and events of the past year emphasize and confirm our previous opinion. Internationally, there has been no trend toward the greater use of silver as a primary monetary metal. It was not mentioned in the tripartite monetary agreement for the stabilization of exchange; China and Hongkong have operated successfully without returning to the silver standard; and Mexico, which re-instated its former silver currency, did so because the prevailing price of the white metal permitted such action to be taken without fear of the melting pot, and presumably because some assurance had been given that the United States would not force the market up to a point where demonetization would again occur." *Ibid.*, 1936, p. 25.

[43] See *Proceedings* of Academy of Political Science, April 1934, Vol. XVI, No. 1, pp. 27–36.

Congress could not possibly bring as much silver into the country as their proponents hoped because, first, silver would not "fly" from India or China, and secondly, because China would place an embargo on silver exports. True, China did place the embargo, but it was ineffective.

He also stated that half the people of the world use silver money, and that if its value were low they would be unable to make purchases abroad. It would have been helpful to apply the same reasoning to the monetary situation of the United States prior to the passage of the Gold Reserve Act of 1934.

Despite all the silver purchased or otherwise added to the nation's stock, and despite the increased volume of certificates, the Government is still far from accomplishing the stated objectives of the Silver Purchase Act. A ratio between the value of silver stocks and gold stocks of 21 percent is still far from 33.3 percent, and Herculean efforts have been required to raise it even that much from the 11 percent ratio which obtained at the time of the Act's passage. (See Chart VII.)

Of the goals which it was sought to achieve through the Silver Purchase Act and through complementary policies of the Government, none has been reached except the increase in price to the domestic producer. But the international negotiations which had to be gone through, the loss of international prestige and goodwill, and the financial chaos perpetrated upon some of the foreign nations are too high a price to pay for such a subsidy to so small a group. While repeal of the Act is not absolutely necessary, at present, taking into consideration the discretionary nature of the power it gives the Executive and the laxity with which it has been prosecuted of late,[44] it would be desirable formally to repeal it. For should some succeeding Administration decide to carry out the law to its full extent, real havoc might ensue. Repeal of a law, however, demands initiative, and it seems unlikely that any one is interested enough to take the initiative needed to introduce a repeal resolution and thus to incur the disfavor of a few silver Senators and the silver interests.

[44] Compare *supra*, p. 74.

IV

THE CHANGED FEDERAL RESERVE NOTE

THE actions of the Roosevelt Administration with respect to Federal Reserve notes should not be considered of great significance as to that Administration's monetary policy. They were merely a continuation of what had been done under the previous Administration. Nevertheless, they are worth noting. The legislation undertaken as to Federal Reserve notes is interesting in that it was the forerunner of the currency-manipulation measures of a little more than a year later, and in that its enactment opened the way to further currency manipulation. It can not be said, of course, that what happened to Federal Reserve notes in 1932 could have served at that time as an omen of what was to come. But analyzing the situation from hindsight, it becomes evident that those operations were only the first steps, halting it is true, toward definite manipulation of the currency in order to achieve some desired economic result outside the purely monetary field.

THE ORIGINAL FEDERAL RESERVE NOTE

Federal Reserve notes, it will be recalled, were the "elastic currency" provided by the Federal Reserve Act of December 23, 1913. The volume of these notes was intended to expand and contract with business activity, and thus to remedy the most glaring defects of the national bank note issue, that of inelasticity and at times of perverse elasticity. The Federal Reserve notes were issued by the Federal Reserve Board (now the Board of Governors of the Federal Reserve System), through the Federal Reserve Agent, in order to meet the currency requirements of the business community. The notes were fully backed by collateral,[1] of which at least 40 percent had to be

[1] "In addition to the collateral against Federal Reserve notes, the Federal Reserve Banks must hold a 5 percent redemption fund in gold with the Treasurer of the United States for such Federal Reserve notes outstanding as are not covered by gold with the Federal Reserve Agents, and a 35 percent reserve in gold or lawful money against their deposits." Federal Reserve Board, *Annual Report,* 1932, pp. 16, 17.

gold or gold certificates, against the Federal Reserve notes in actual circulation, and the remainder, up to 60 percent, could consist of eligible paper bought or discounted by the specific Federal Reserve Bank involved. Eligible paper included commercial, agricultural, and industrial paper, and paper secured by United States Government obligations rediscounted by member banks with the Reserve Banks, member bank collateral notes secured by eligible paper or by obligations of the United States Government, and bankers' acceptances purchased by the Reserve Banks. If there was a deficiency of such paper, then gold had to be used as backing.

INSUFFICIENCY OF ELIGIBLE PAPER

During the course of the depression a paucity of eligible paper in some banks did develop,[2] and, as a consequence, the amount of gold necessary to serve as collateral for the Federal Reserve notes had to be increased. Indeed, the proportion rose so that at times the Federal Reserve notes were almost gold certificates. The ratio of gold and gold certificates to notes issued[3] rose from 91 percent at the end of January, 1931, to 94 percent on July 31, 1931, a figure which has been equaled and even surpassed since then, but which was considered very high at that time.

Furthermore, the increased hoarding of Federal Reserve notes, along with other types of currency, during this period, prevented the true "elasticity" character of the notes from making itself felt. That is, instead of the amount of Federal Reserve notes outstanding showing a decline during the depression, as it was theoretically supposed to do, it continued to expand. This expansion was caused not by business needs, obviously, but by the hoarding engendered by fear of the banking system and by the general business recession then in progress.

Consequently, the Federal Reserve Banks had to find something else to serve as backing for their notes, especially if there

[2] True, the member banks could have rediscounted, with the Federal Reserve Banks, their own notes backed by Government obligations. But that would have made it more difficult, if not impossible, for the Reserve System to pursue its easy-money goal.

[3] Notes issued, of course, total more than notes in circulation so that the ratios here quoted are understated to some extent.

should be an external drain of gold, such as was experienced in the autumn of 1931, and again in the spring of 1932.[4] The amount of gold withdrawn in September and October, 1931, following upon England's abandonment of the gold standard on September 21, 1931, amounted to $725,000,000. Although reversal of the outflow occurred in November and December, the monetary gold stock at the end of 1931 was $133,000,000 less than at the beginning of the year.

The net outflow of gold was resumed in January and February, 1932, during which months the United States lost $44,000,000 and $62,000,000, respectively. It was at that time that there began to appear computations of the amount of "free" gold in the nation. The Federal Reserve Board gave an explanation as follows:[5]

Excess reserves and free gold.—It is on these provisions[6] of the law that calculations of the Federal Reserve Banks' excess reserves and of their free gold were based. Excess reserves are the total reserves of the Reserve Banks less the 40 percent gold reserve against Federal Reserve notes and the 35 percent gold or lawful money reserve against deposits. Collateral requirements do not enter into the calculations of excess reserves. The term free gold, on the other hand, meant gold held by the Reserve Banks that was not required either as reserves or as collateral for Federal Reserve notes.

The position of the Reserve Banks in regard to excess reserves and free gold since January 1929 is shown in the chart [not re-

[4] "During the fiscal year 1932 the resources of the Federal Reserve Banks were brought to the support of the country's banking system. Unprecedented demands upon our gold stock following the suspension of the gold standard in England in September, together with a continued domestic withdrawal of currency, chiefly for hoarding, were met by the Reserve Banks through discount and open-market operations, but nevertheless the pressure upon our banking system was reflected in firm conditions in the money market at the end of 1931 and the beginning of 1932. After the turn of the year as constructive and remedial measures were formulated and brought into operation and as the Federal Reserve System at the end of February engaged in open-market purchases of United States securities on a large scale, money market conditions became easier. Reserve Bank rates, which had been increased during the autumn of 1931, were again reduced, as money rates in the open market declined. By the middle of September, 1932, short-term money rates in the open market were again at the low levels reached in the previous summer." Secretary of the Treasury, *Annual Report,* 1932, p. 64.

[5] *Annual Report,* 1932, pp. 17, 18.

[6] See *supra,* pp. 81, 82.

produced here], which indicates that when section 3 of the Glass-Steagall Act became effective the distinction between excess reserves and free gold lost its significance.

On February 24, 1932, the Federal Reserve Banks had $1,392,000,000 of excess reserves, but as they did not have a sufficient amount of eligible paper available as collateral, $930,000,000 of these excess reserves in the form of gold had to be pledged as collateral against Federal Reserve notes, in addition to $46,000,000 required for the redemption fund, with the consequence that the gold not needed for these purposes amounted to $416,000,000.

Among the factors combining to reduce the amount of "free" gold were the following: open-market purchases of Governments by the Federal Reserve Banks; the low volume of acceptances; the growth in the volume of Federal Reserve notes outstanding, due of course to hoarding; and the large volume of gold exports.

PASSAGE OF THE GLASS-STEAGALL ACT

With excitement bordering on panic, and after hearings and debates, it was decided to permit the substitution of Government securities for gold as collateral backing for Federal Reserve notes, but only above the 40 percent gold minimum required. The Bill, later passed as the Glass-Steagall Act, was introduced into the Senate by Senator Glass, and into the House by Representative Steagall. The Bill was signed by President Hoover and duly became law on February 27, 1932. Provisions in the Act, dealing with purely banking operations in contradistinction to its monetary aspects, will not be touched upon here.

The last section of the Act, that dealing with the backing for Federal Reserve notes, states that "until March 3, 1933, should the Federal Reserve Board deem it in the public interest, it may, upon the affirmative vote of not less than a majority of its members, authorize the Federal Reserve Banks to offer, and the Federal Reserve Agents to accept, as such collateral security [against Federal Reserve notes] direct obligations of the United States."

It is thus seen that the Glass-Steagall Act did not change the 100 percent collateral requirement, but merely changed the type of collateral that could be eligible. Instead of only gold and "eligible" paper, as previously. United States Government obligations also, even those purchased in the open market by the Federal Reserve Banks, could serve as Reserve-note backing.

This provision did not broaden the lending facilities of the Reserve Banks, but it did increase their power to make open-market purchases of Governments. Thus they could offset the gold exports and the currency drains on the one hand, and increase member-bank reserves on the other. These reserves could be used either to repay borrowings at the Reserve Banks or to increase loans and investments.

Following the passage of the Act, the Reserve Banks increased their holdings of United States Governments by about $1,000,000,000. During the same period, the outflow of gold amounted to $500,000,000, and member banks were enabled to reduce their borrowings from the Reserve Banks by $350,-000,000 and at the same time to raise their reserves by $200,-000,000. Thus the Federal Reserve Board was able to conclude[7] that "the enactment of legislation that enables the Federal Reserve system to pursue a policy based on the assurance that in case of need not merely its 'free gold' will be available, but practically its entire gold reserve in excess of legal requirements, has resulted in strengthening the entire credit structure of the country and in increasing the system's power to coöperate in the recovery of business."

United States Government securities were first pledged on May 5, 1932. The largest amount used as collateral at any one time during 1932 was $682,000,000 (on July 6), and the amount on December 31, 1932, had fallen to $428,000,000. At the end of May, 1932, $205,000,000 of Governments were held as collateral behind Federal Reserve notes issued. A month later the figure had jumped to $635,000,000, a month-end figure which was exceeded only during the Bank Holiday of 1933. At the end of March, 1933, Governments behind the notes totaled almost $900,000,000 and were equal to 22 percent of notes issued. Neither of these figures has been approached since. Governments now total only $25,000,000, and represent but

[7] *Federal Reserve Bulletin,* March, 1932, p. 144.

one-half percent of notes issued. Indeed, the seeming ineffectiveness of the Glass-Steagall provisions, at present, is evidenced by the fact that on several occasions recently gold certificates behind notes issued were equal to more than 100 percent of the notes issued. (See Chart IX.) But this view, that the amend-

Chart IX

FEDERAL RESERVE NOTES ISSUED, AND RATIO OF COLLATERAL TO ISSUE

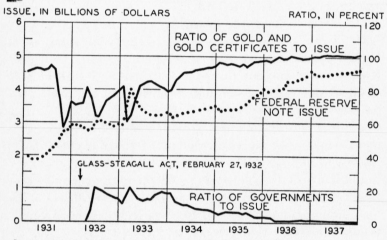

Source: Board of Governors of the Federal Reserve System.

ment is readily dispensable, is not concurred in by the Chairman of the Board of Governors of the Federal Reserve System.[8]

EXTENSION OF THE GLASS-STEAGALL ACT

Before the year elapsed during which the original Glass-Steagall Act was to run its course, Congress extended the provisions to March 3, 1934, by an Act of February 3, 1933. A year later, when the new Administration was seeking all means possible to secure and maintain control of the monetary system, the appeal of the flexibility provided by the Glass-Steagall amendment to the Federal Reserve Act could not be resisted. On March 6, 1934, the Act was extended again, to March 3,

[8] See next page.

1935, with the provision that the President could extend the term of its effectiveness for two years longer. As expected, the President did extend the period. On February 14, 1935, he issued a proclamation extending for the full two years allowed —that is, until March 3, 1937—the period within which the Federal Reserve Board could authorize the Federal Reserve Banks to offer and the Federal Reserve Agents to accept direct obligations of the United States as collateral security for Federal Reserve notes, for that portion above the 40 percent amount of gold reserve required.

On March 1, 1937, the President signed still another law to "extend the period during which direct obligations of the United States may be used as collateral security for Federal Reserve notes" to June 30, 1939. Chairman Eccles, of the Board of Governors of the Federal Reserve System, had made a plea on February 16, 1937, before the House Banking and Currency Committee, to continue this provision so that the Reserve System would not be forced to adopt "a restrictive credit policy" leading to deflation. The reason he gave was that, due to the insufficiency of eligible paper, gold up to 100 percent would have to be used by some of the Federal Reserve Banks to back their notes, and since several of them lacked enough gold for this purpose they would be forced to sell their Governments. He said that this policy had no relation to the increase in required reserves, nor would it conflict with the Treasury's gold "sterilization" operations.

GOLD CERTIFICATES REPLACE GOLD

One more item should be mentioned with respect to Federal Reserve notes. That is the amendment substituting gold certificates for gold as collateral for the notes. The Gold Reserve Act of 1934 amended the Federal Reserve Act (section 16) so as to make Federal Reserve notes redeemable only in lawful money. It also eliminated the use of gold (but not gold certificates) as collateral for Federal Reserve notes, and required that reserves against Federal Reserve notes should henceforth be maintained in gold certificates instead. Also, reserves against deposits in Federal Reserve Banks were to be maintained in gold certificates or lawful money instead of in gold or lawful money. In addition, the Act required the redemption fund of the Federal Reserve Banks, deposited with the Treasurer of the United States, to be in gold certificates instead of in gold, and that all deposits of Federal Reserve Banks and Federal Reserve Agents with the Treasurer were to be repayable in gold certificates only and not in gold coins. Thus, the collateral behind

Chart X

FEDERAL RESERVE NOTES IN CIRCULATION, AS PERCENTAGE OF TOTAL
MONEY IN CIRCULATION

(At End of Each Quarter)

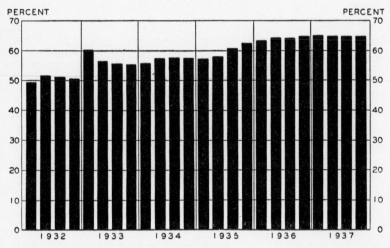

Source: United States Treasury Department.

Federal Reserve notes now consists of the following only: gold certificates, eligible paper, and Government securities.

INCREASING IMPORTANCE OF THE FEDERAL RESERVE NOTE

The changing importance of Federal Reserve notes in the total monetary circulation in the United States is illustrated by the following figures on the proportion of the circulation represented by Federal Reserve notes: first quarter of 1932, 49 percent; second quarter of 1935 (just preceding the beginning of the retirement of national bank notes), 58 percent; end of

1937, 65 percent. That is, Federal Reserve notes accounted for just under half the total monetary circulation in early 1932, and in the next five or six years rose to two-thirds of the circulation. Chart X shows the steadily rising trend of the proportion of these notes in the first five years of the period and stability in the last, which resulted from the increased circulation of silver certificates, as shown in Chart XII. Silver dollars and silver certificates constituted 7½ percent of circulation at the end of the first quarter of 1932, and rose to 18 percent of total by December 31, 1937.

V
THE PASSING OF THE NATIONAL BANK NOTE

ONE phase of the Roosevelt Administration's currency policies with which no monetary economist can find fault is the abolition of the national bank notes. The various shortcomings of the national bank notes, such as inelasticity, perverse elasticity, and the like, are too familiar to require comment here.

Their abolition has been sought since the early days of the century, an operation which the passage of the Federal Reserve Act of 1913 seemed almost to guarantee. Far from such elimination being a certainty, however, the circulation of national bank notes, which had amounted to $715,754,000 on June 30, 1913, actually rose higher than that amount time and again during the twenties, and at the beginning of the depression of the thirties still stood at more than $650,000,000. The enlarged circulation during the three years beginning August, 1932, was due to special circumstances, which are further described below.

BONDS BEARING THE "CIRCULATION PRIVILEGE"

Until the depression there were only two series of United States bonds which bore the "circulation privilege"—the 2 percent Consols of 1930, and the two series of 2 percent Panama Canal bonds of 1916–36 and 1918–38. The 2 percent Consols of 1930 were "payable at the pleasure of the United States" after April 1, 1930. Because of their circulation privilege, however, the Secretary of the Treasury announced, on December 12, 1929, that they would not be called for redemption on April 2, 1930, "the earliest date the option reserved to the United States may be exercised," thus formally extending the term of their life indefinitely.

Of the $646,000,000 of 2 percent Consols which had been issued, about $600,000,000 were still outstanding on June 30, 1935. The 2 percent Panama Canal loans issued in 1906 and

1908 were redeemable after August 1, 1916, and November 1, 1918, respectively, and were to mature on August 1, 1936, and November 1, 1938, respectively. The original issues of these 2 percent Panama Canal bonds totaled $85,000,000, and on June 30, 1935, $75,000,000 worth were still outstanding.[1]

EXTENDING THE CIRCULATION PRIVILEGE

A "rider" to the Federal Home Loan Bank Act of July 22, 1932, as an emergency measure, amended the National Bank Act by making all United States Government bonds bearing coupon rates up to $3\frac{3}{8}$ percent eligible as security for circulation of national bank notes. Thus, national banks which owned such Government bonds were able to obtain currency without selling or borrowing on these securities. This provision, however, was to remain in effect for three years only, and automatically terminated on July 21, 1935.

While theoretically the increased collateral thus made available for backing national bank notes enlarged the potential national bank note issue by more than $3,000,000,000, actually only about $900,000,000 additional could be issued. This was because of the limitation with respect to paid-in capital stock.[2] But even this $900,000,000 disturbed the Secretary of the Treasury. He admitted that the additional issue may have been helpful in some localities, but he deplored the fact that the banks could issue an additional total amount up to $900,000,000. Under different business and economic conditions, he claimed,

---

[1] "The 2 percent consols in the amount of $646,250,150 were issued between 1900 and 1907 under the Act of March 14, 1900, in refunding a like amount of outstanding 3, 4, and 5 percent bonds. Under section 18 of the Federal Reserve Act $46,526,100 of the consols were refunded into 3 percent bonds and notes, reducing the amount outstanding to $599,724,050, the amount called. Two percent bonds, in the amount of $84,631,980, were issued under the Act of June 28, 1902, to provide funds for the construction of the Panama Canal. These bonds were issued in two series, $54,631,980, dated August 1, 1906 making up the series of 1916–36, and $30,000,000, dated November 1, 1908, making up the series of 1918–38. Under the Federal Reserve Act, $5,677,800 of the former and $4,052,600 of the latter series were refunded into 3 percent bonds or notes, reducing the amounts outstanding to $48,954,180 and $25,947,400, respectively." Secretary of the Treasury, *Annual Report*, 1935, p. 22.

[2] "By this Act the circulation privilege was extended to an additional $3,089,-000,000 of United States bonds. At the end of the three-year period the notes issued against such bonds must be retired in an appropriate manner. The out-

the power of the banks to issue such an amount of additional notes would seriously interfere with the Federal Reserve System's contact with the market and its ability to influence credit conditions.

WITHDRAWAL OF THE CIRCULATION PRIVILEGE

On March 11, 1935, the Secretary of the Treasury announced plans to retire the Treasury's 2 percent Consols and the 2 percent Panama Canal loan bonds through the use of $642,000,000 "free gold"[3] resulting from devaluation of the gold dollar. He called the 2 percent Consols of 1930 as of July 1, 1935, and the 2 percent Panama Canal bonds as of August 1, 1935. Thus, as a result of this call, coupled with the expiration of the emergency amendment of July 22, 1932, all provision for national bank-note issue would cease by August 1, 1935. The retirement of these bonds and the expiration of the authority to use other bonds as backing for national bank notes would result in the eventual elimination of national bank notes as a medium of circulation and would accomplish a simplification of the currency system of the United States.

---

standing bond issues accorded the circulation privilege by the new legislation are the following:

	Outstanding June 30, 1932 (In thousands)
2½ percent postal savings bonds (3d to 42d series)	$36,247
3 percent conversion bonds of 1946–47	28,895
3 percent Panama Canal loan of 1961	49,800
3 percent Treasury bonds of 1951–55	800,422
3⅛ percent Treasury bonds of 1946–49	821,403
3⅜ percent Treasury bonds of 1940–43	352,994
3⅜ percent Treasury bonds of 1941–43	544,917
3⅜ percent Treasury bonds of 1943–47	454,135
Total	$3,088,813

"The maximum amount of national bank notes which may be issued under the new authorization is limited by the provision of the National Bank Act which precludes a national bank from issuing notes in excess of its paid-in capital. On June 30, 1932, the paid-in capital stock of active national banks was $1,570,000,000 and national bank notes secured by United States bonds were outstanding in the amount of $670,000,000 leaving $900,000,000 as the additional amount of notes which may be issued under the new legislation." Secretary of the Treasury, *Annual Report*, 1932, p. 72.

[3] Gold-dollar devaluation "profit" not otherwise earmarked or used. Not to be confused with the "free gold" in the Federal Reserve System, prior to 1932. See p. 83.

The immediate steps in the process of retiring the national bank notes consisted in the assumption by the Treasury of liability for those notes, as the national banks deposited funds with the Treasurer for their redemption. Theoretically the process was as follows. A national bank would take a Consol (say) to the Treasurer, turn it in and receive its money, and immediately give the funds it had received back to the Treasurer for the latter to use in the redemption of that bank's outstanding notes. The bank thus wiped out a liability (national bank notes outstanding) by paying out an asset (Consols), leaving its net position unchanged. Actually, of course, some deposits were made with the Treasurer before the bonds were redeemed.[4]

The final stage in the actual redemption is as follows. When the Federal Reserve Banks ship unfit national bank notes to the Treasury for retirement, payment is made by a charge against the Treasury's account at the Reserve Banks. As the Treasury replenishes its account at the Reserve Banks by depositing gold certificates, based upon the gold increment aris-

[4] "From early in March, when the bonds were called, to the end of June [1935] national banks deposited with the United States Treasury about $410,-000,000 of funds, thereby transferring to the Treasury the liability for redeeming these notes upon return from circulation. During this period about $90,-000,000 of national bank notes were retired, largely as they became unfit for further circulation and were returned to the Treasury. The difference between these two amounts, $320,000,000, represented funds temporarily placed at the disposal of the Treasury. These funds were not specifically earmarked but were placed in the general-fund balance of the Treasury.

"The next stage in the elimination of national bank notes from the circulating medium of the country was the retirement of the bonds. On July 1, national banks which still had national bank notes outstanding against the pledge of consols were allowed to offset this liability against amounts due to them for redeemed consols and against balances remaining in their redemption fund with the Treasury applicable to these notes. Funds needed by the Treasury to redeem consols were acquired principally by withdrawals from depositary banks. As a result, these transactions were completed without any significant change in aggregate member bank reserve balances. The expiration of the temporary circulation privilege on July 22 necessitated the deposit of funds with the Treasury to cover the liability for national bank notes secured by these bonds. Since no bonds matured on this date the only offsetting item consisted of the relatively small balance remaining in the redemption fund applicable to notes outstanding against these bonds. Practically all of these transactions were completed prior to July 22. The redemption of Panamas on August 1 required the same sort of transactions as the redemption of consols, but the amounts involved were much smaller." Board of Governors of the Federal Reserve System, *Annual Report*, 1935, pp. 27, 28.

ing from the revaluation of the dollar, retirement of the national bank notes is thus effected without reduction either in member bank reserve balances or in the Treasury's cash balance.

As explained above, part of the "profit" resulting from the reduction in the weight of the gold dollar was to be used for the retirement of the bonds bearing the permanent circulation privilege. But "in order to avoid any temporary alteration in the aggregate supply of money" by these operations, it was decided to deposit gold certificates against gold representing this part of the increment in the Federal Reserve Banks only as rapidly as approximately corresponding amounts of national bank notes were retired. These gold certificates would increase the reserves against which Federal Reserve notes could be issued in replacement of the national bank currency retired. Also, obviously, the excess-reserves situation, already beginning to show danger signals, would not be further aggravated.

RETIREMENT OF NATIONAL BANK NOTES

The disappearance of national bank notes from circulation has proved to be a slow process. On December 31, 1937, almost three years after the commencement of their final retirement, there were still outstanding almost $250,000,000 of national bank notes. (See Charts XI and XII.) True, they were technically no longer the same national bank notes as those outstanding previous to mid-1935; that is, instead of being bond-backed 100 percent plus a 5 percent redemption fund, they were backed entirely by cash already turned in to the Treasury, which now became responsible for them. In fact, the Treasury's non-interest-bearing debt, consisting mainly of the deposits by the national banks for the retirement of their bank notes, was increased by $800,000,000 on this account in July, 1935. By December, 1937, this figure had fallen to about $275,-000,000 indicating that only that amount of national bank notes and Federal Reserve bank notes was still in circulation and merely awaiting presentation to the Treasury to be redeemed and permanently retired from the monetary system of the United States.

As stated above, the redemption of the bank notes was to be effected, in large part, through the proceeds from the increment resulting from the reduction in the weight of the gold dollar, i. e., from the gold-dollar devaluation "profit."[5] By December 31, 1937, $618,000,000 had been utilized for this purpose. Also, while $250,000,000 of notes were still outstanding, there was left of the gold "profit" only about $160,000,000, indicating thus that the Treasury would have to draw upon its general funds to the extent of $90,000,000 in order to complete the redemption process. In addition, of course, there are the Fed-

Chart XI

NATIONAL BANK NOTES IN CIRCULATION

(At End of Each Month. Outside the Treasury and the Federal Reserve Banks)

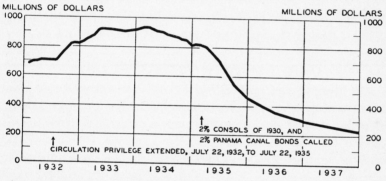

Source: United States Treasury Department.

eral Reserve bank notes which are also in process of redemption. However, funds had already been deposited to take care of these redemptions, so that any draft upon the general fund will constitute merely repayment of moneys it had already borrowed, as it were, from the redemption fund.

NATIONAL BANK NOTES REPLACED BY FEDERAL RESERVE NOTES AND SILVER CERTIFICATES

The Secretary of the Treasury stated, when he made the bond-redemption calls, that the retirement of the national

[5] For disposition of the "profit," see *supra*, p. 29.

bank notes would simplify the currency issues of the United States.[6] He also said that Federal Reserve notes would soon replace the retired national bank notes, thus avoiding any net change in the total of money in circulation. The Secretary of the Treasury, deliberately or otherwise, forgot to state that a large part of the gap in the currency which might have resulted from the redemption of the bank notes would be filled in by the silver certificates then in process of being issued. This type of currency in circulation rose from close to $400,000,000 on June 30, 1934, to more than $1,100,000,000, on December 31, 1937, while national bank notes had fallen during that same period from $900,000,000 to $250,000,000. Federal Reserve notes too had risen, from less than $3,100,000,000 on June 30, 1934, to almost $4,300,000,000 on December 31, 1937. Thus the retirement of national bank notes may theoretically be said to have been offset by the increase in silver certificates, while the increase in the total volume of money in circulation, of $1,190,000,000, was met in largest part by the increase in Federal Reserve notes outstanding. (See Chart XII.)

With the passing of the national bank notes, the United States lost much of the difference between the national banking system and the state banking systems. Except for automatic membership in the Federal Reserve System, different examining boards, and more or less different standards of examination, appraisal, and the like, the main point of differentiation between the national banking system and any strict state banking system, as in New York State, was formerly the privilege of currency issue. The power to receive time (savings) deposits, the authority to engage in trust and fiduciary operations, and the privilege to engage to some extent in real-estate financing, were enjoyed by national banks as well as by the specifically state-chartered institutions. Only as regards the note issue did they diverge. An obvious question now relevant is what is the use of the two, or one might say, the fifty commercial banking

---

[6] "National bank notes, which have been an important part of this country's circulating medium since the establishment of the national banking system in 1863, are now being gradually retired from circulation. Their eventual disappearance will constitute a step in the simplification of our currrency system." Secretary of the Treasury, *Annual Report*, 1936, p. 46.

systems? Why not unify and make only one system, and that a federally chartered and controlled one, for all states and the District of Columbia? However, this problem is outside the scope of this study. I merely wished to mention it, without attempting to suggest any approach to, or actual solution of, the problem.

Although the step taken by the Administration with respect to national bank notes was one which had been sought for a long time by monetary economists, it was not a major move in

Chart XII

MONEY IN CIRCULATION, BY TYPES

(At End of Each Month. Outside the Treasury and the Federal Reserve Banks)

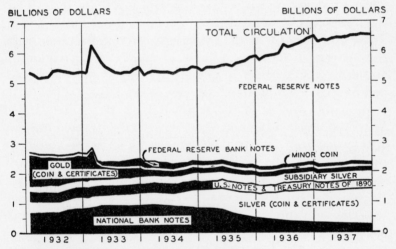

Source: United States Treasury Department.

the Administration's monetary policies. True, it tended to centralize direct control of the currency still more in the Federal Reserve System, but the increased issuance of silver certificates acted somewhat as an offset by permitting a certain amount of control to the Treasury. On the other hand, though, in a nation whose chief means of payment consists of check and deposit currency, monetary management is effected not only through control of monetary and currency paper, but also through control of the credit machinery.

VI

FEDERAL RESERVE BANK NOTES AND OTHER MISCELLANEOUS CURRENCY

FROM the very start, Federal Reserve bank notes seem to have been an emergency currency. They were first issued in 1916. The Secretary of the Treasury reported that on February 1 of that year there were outstanding $1,000,000 of Federal Reserve bank notes. By June 30, $1,683,000 were outstanding. They became of real importance, however, only with the passage of the Pittman Act of 1918.[1] That Act authorized the conversion of silver coin into bullion, in order to provide silver for export balances to ship to the Orient.

The melting-down of the bullion necessitated the withdrawal of silver certificates from circulation. These were replaced by Federal Reserve bank notes of the same value, backed by short-term Federal Government obligations. The total amount of certificates retired was about $250,000,000. After the war emergency, the Treasury was to retire the Federal Reserve bank notes by purchasing silver and issuing silver certificates in their stead, to the amount of silver melted down in the interim. This was done during the period extending to mid-1923, when the Treasury completed its purchase of Pittman Act silver.

The Federal Reserve bank notes were expected to die a lingering death, and by June 30, 1932, seemed well on the way to extinction. On that date, $2,746,000 only were still outstanding. But the Emergency Banking Act of March 9, 1933, changed the picture entirely by broadening the authority of the Federal Reserve Banks to issue such notes.

The backing for these bank notes was provided under what was known at the time as the "cats and dogs" clause, because it permitted almost anything to serve as backing, not excepting,

[1] Act of April 2, 1918: "An Act to conserve the gold supply of the United States; to permit the settlement in silver of trade balances adverse to the United States; to provide silver for subsidiary coinage and for commercial use; to assist foreign governments at war with the enemies of the United States; and for the above purposes to stabilize the price and encourage the production of silver."

perhaps, even the "paper on the wall." The Federal Reserve bank notes issued under authority of this Act could be issued against any direct obligations of the United States, or against the security of any notes, drafts, exchanges, or bankers' acceptances. The issue backed by the former could amount to 100 percent of the collateral, while notes backed by the latter were allowable only up to 90 percent of the estimated value of the collateral tendered.

The amount of Federal Reserve bank notes in circulation rose from $3,000,000 on February 28, 1933, to a month-end peak of $208,000,000 on December 31, 1933. The gradual retirement since then has resulted in an outstanding total of little more than $30,000,000, on December 31, 1937. (See Chart XII.) Even these, moreover, have all had money deposited with the Treasurer of the United States for their redemption when they are turned in from circulation.

It is difficult to understand the reasoning behind the authorization of the issue of Federal Reserve bank notes. Federal Reserve notes, under the Glass-Steagall amendment to the Federal Reserve Act,[2] could be issued against United States obligations, and even before that amendment—that is, under the Federal Reserve Act as originally passed—they were issued against eligible commercial paper. Hence, they differed from this new type of Federal Reserve bank notes, if at all, only in the probable ease and laxness which was expected to attend their issue. Of course, the state of panic which prevailed throughout the nation in the first week and a half of March, 1933, gave birth to many superfluities and the new Federal Reserve bank notes were probably but one, and only a minor one, in a long line of such excesses.

The final retirement of Federal Reserve bank notes again seems on the road to consummation, but any slight emergency might easily call a halt to this process. It is unlikely that there will be such need, however, especially in view of the recurrent extensions to the active life of the Glass-Steagall amendment of 1932 and the ever-increasing importance of the silver certificates.

[2] See *supra*, p. 84, *et seq.*

238694

TREASURY NOTES OF 1890

The Treasury notes of 1890 are secured dollar for dollar by standard silver dollars held in the Treasury. These notes are being retired and canceled upon receipt by the Treasury, according to a statement by the Secretary of the Treasury. Of late they have been of small significance in our monetary system. At no time since 1916 has their total issue amounted to even $2,000,000. As of December 31, 1937, there were only $1,170,572 still outstanding. The Roosevelt Administration had originated no definite policy in regard to these notes, merely redeeming them as they came in. Then again, the silver certificates now issued match them in almost every respect, differing only as to name, and as to date of issue.

THE "GREENBACKS"

The United States notes, or "Greenbacks," totaling $346,-681,016 now outstanding, must be reissued when redeemed. They are backed by a gold reserve of $156,039,430.93. This gold reserve also stands back of the Treasury notes of 1890, but the latter provision is of no significance because of the silver reserve behind those notes. United States notes were first authorized by the Act of February 25, 1862, and subsequent acts either increased the amounts permitted to be outstanding or halted their redemption, a process which the Treasury had been vigorously pursuing. The total amount authorized to be outstanding at any time was $450,000,000. The greatest amount outstanding at any one time, $449,338,902, was reached on January 30, 1864. Two laws, one passed in 1866 and one in 1868, provided for the gradual retirement of these notes. An act in 1873, however, directed the reissuance of $26,000,000 "in response to popular demand." The Resumption Act of 1875 ordered a reduction in outstanding to $300,000,000, but in 1878 Congress ordered that process to cease, and that the Treasury reissue notes upon their redemption. At that time $346,681,016 was outstanding, and this amount has continued to the present. (See Chart XII.)

The New Deal Administration appears to have missed a good opportunity to rid the nation of these notes, and thus to further the "simplification of the currency," as it enthusiastically did with national bank notes. The Administration's decision to continue them in existence may have rested upon the fact that the Treasury would have had to lay out $190,641,585.07 for redeeming that portion of the United States notes not backed by gold. This would have been a small price to pay, however, to get rid of the notes. Indeed, some of the seigniorage from silver, or the remainder, if any, of the "profit" from gold dollar devaluation could very well have been used for this purpose, without even disturbing the ordinary finances of the Government. Also, the gross public debt would have been cut by the amount of the issue.

In connection with United States notes, mention should be made of a provision in the "Thomas" Inflation Amendment of May 12, 1933. This provision has not been made use of as yet. It authorizes the issuance of United States notes as pure fiat currency up to $3,000,000,000, if the Federal Reserve System should not "coöperate," when requested, by purchasing an additional $3,000,000,000 of United States obligations in the open market in furtherance of the aims *then* current— greater monetary circulation, therefore higher prices, therefore recovery. As stated by the Secretary of the Treasury,[3]

The [amendment] gave broad authority to the President, upon determination of the existence of certain conditions, to require the Secretary of the Treasury to enter into agreements with the Federal Reserve Banks and the Federal Reserve Board for the purchase of additional United States obligations in an aggregate sum of $3,000,000,000 and, under certain conditions and limitations, to require the issuance of United States notes—not to exceed $3,000,000,000 to be outstanding at any one time—for the purpose of meeting maturing Federal obligations and of purchasing interest-bearing obligations of the United States.

This provision would have little practical interest except for a statement by a member of the Board of Governors of the Federal Reserve System. Mr. Chester C. Davis, in a speech to the Montana Bankers' Association, on June 25, 1937, posed the following as one question, among many others, "about

[3] Secretary of the Treasury, *Annual Report,* 1933, pp. 25, 26.

which people ought to be thinking": "Should the government abandon the almost universal practice of issuing interest-bearing bonds when it borrows on credit, and turn to the issuance of non-interest-bearing notes in their stead?" Thus he seemingly advocates the substitution of currency issues for bonds and other interest-bearing obligations in order, for example, to finance a deficit by fiat money. But this is a rock upon which any fiscal and financial system will come to wreck. Whether anything will come of such a suggestion remains to be seen, but its mere utterance by a responsible member of the agency which is supposed to control the banking and credit structure of the nation indicates, apparently, that it was not without significance, and thus merits attention and more than passing thought.

VII

APPRAISAL OF THE MONETARY POLICIES

WHEN viewed in the mass, the monetary policies of the United States in the years 1932 to 1937 appear to be but a conglomerate of short, staccato steps. The steps have not always been taken in the same direction, even though the policies underlying them did allegedly have in view some rather vague goals connected with price-raising and with recovery in internal activity and foreign trade. Some of the steps taken were definitely aimed at these goals, while others were taken in exactly the opposite direction. In justification it can perhaps be said that the exigencies of the moment demanded certain steps, and that the steps were but fluctuations, as it were, about a main line of trend. Some of the drives toward the goals may be said to have gone a shade too fast, and thus were above the main line of trend, while others were too slow, and thus below the trendline. Although it would be intellectually satisfying to be able to accept this reasoning sequence, it would be straining a point to do so.

POLITICAL PRESSURE

Each step in the monetary field was taken not only as part of the general striving toward the goals enumerated above, but also as a result of political prodding by one or another pressure-group. These pressure-groups at times were composed of agriculturalists, then of silver speculators, then of foreign traders, and so on. It may be true that a democracy can function only with the assistance of such pressure-groups. But one cannot complacently condone the brushing aside of expert and studied advice, and the acceptance of counsel from minority groups, all of which have an axe to grind. That the present Administration has been especially prone to accept such biased advice is seen by its actions in the monetary field, which show plainly how first one pressure-group held sway, to be replaced by another, which in turn would be scrapped for still another.

MONEY IN A PRICE-PROFIT ECONOMY

The importance of the monetary system in a business and profit economy, such as obtains in the United States, should give one pause before undertaking to tamper with it as a means of securing some desired economic end. True, if the right remedy be applied the success would undoubtedly be great, but the chances of failure also are very great. History is replete with examples of well-intentioned attempts to use monetary means to cure all economic ills. Definite promise may have been made that such means were going to be used in moderation only and would not be allowed to over-reach the limit of tolerance—still less even to approach the devastating stage of affairs on the other side of that limit. But, time and again, that limit was reached and passed. Examples are so many and so well-known that even the citing of them would be useless repetition.

While not denying the all-pervading importance of the monetary system, it should not be forgotten that other phenomena also assume a significant part in motivating the economy. In addition to financial factors other than monetary, there are technical, industrial factors to be considered, as well as the stage of industrial progress. Nor can the state of political and international affairs be dismissed. Hence, it is difficult to conclude that manipulation of only one phase of this total economic set-up—for example, the monetary phase—can result in setting aright a whole economic system which has gone awry. Should an attempt be made to control the total economy, then obviously the monetary branch must be controlled too, in order to render effective the correlative controls. But that is not what the extremists of the monetary manipulators desire. They believe that by changing the numbers upon the nation's coin and currency a central authority can, at will, move the economic structure *in toto*.

When the Roosevelt Administration took over the reins of Government in March, 1933, the financial paralysis in the nation was symbolic of the general house cleaning needed in the banking and financial parts of the economic structure. The stress of events at the time called for immediate action of some kind. The form of action most readily at hand was the temporary closing-down of the whole financial system in order to give the new Administration opportunity to develop more nearly permanent remedies. One may or may not agree that such wholesale closing was the best action to take, but, right or wrong, it did focus attention upon the inherent disabilities and weaknesses of the system. The fault that the author finds in that step is that it opened too free a way for later monetary manipulation. Under the plea of emergency, fundamental changes were made in the monetary structure, changes which should have been made, if at all, only after carefully considered study and with as little haste as possible. But the widespread activities of the Roosevelt Administration in the monetary field, during only the first year and a half of its rule, touched upon all but the most minor types of money—that is, it touched upon gold, silver, Federal Reserve notes, Federal Reserve bank notes, national bank notes, and United States notes. Only the Treasury notes of 1890 and the subsidiary coinage were neglected in the general overhauling.

APPRAISAL OF THE GOLD POLICY

The gold embargo first imposed under the Proclamation of March 6, 1933, was an emergency measure and should have remained so. Its continuance after the first few days or weeks of the emergency was undesirable, and in view of the happenings since January, 1934, this continuance is seen to have been entirely unnecessary. The gold export embargo, in fact, has no place in the United States; rather would it have been preferable during the period under review to place an *import* embargo.

The calling-in of gold by the Federal Government was probably a good thing. If gold is so valuable, and if, over the long period, it is becoming comparatively scarce, then it is just as well that it be preserved from wearing out or disappearing in any other way, especially when paper and other forms of currency are able to assume the monetary functions more cheaply and as efficiently.

The professed main reason for varying the price of gold and devaluing the gold dollar was "to restore commodity price levels," and upon restoration of the level, "to establish and maintain a dollar which will not change its purchasing and debt-paying power during the succeeding generation." An added excuse was "to protect the foreign commerce of the United States against the adverse effect of depreciated foreign currencies."

Wholesale commodity prices did rise—by 47 percent, from February, 1933, to April, 1937. But one-third of the rise had occurred in the early summer months of 1933, after which a rather slow but comparatively steady increase was experienced until early 1937. Toward the middle of 1937, commodity prices began to decline and at the end of the year were 7 percent below the high. The recent decline in commodity prices is thus seen to have taken place concurrently with the business recession of the autumn and winter of 1937–1938; and it took place, too, with no change in the mint price of gold. Prices have risen throughout the world, also, but United States monetary policy cannot be given all the credit for increasing world prices, or even for the increasing[1] American price level.

Agricultural prices rose partly as a result of a series of devastating droughts which occurred not only in the United States, but also in other nations. In addition, restricted production in pursuit of Agricultural Adjustment Administration policies, coupled with actual destruction of food and other agricultural products, were bound to have price repercussions.

Industrial prices rose not because of the gold policies, but the rise stemmed rather from National Industrial Recovery Administration policies, which, among other things, increased costs; then too, world-wide industrial recovery also stimulated industrial prices. Industrial recovery in the United States until recently had gone on apace, too, but increasing the price of gold cannot be credited with being the motivating force. It apparently did not head off the 1937–1938 recession.

Foreign trade has shown some recovery from depression levels, but the amount of recovery which is due to gold manipulation is probably not measurable. Especially is this so when consideration is given to the defense measures undertaken by

[1] Until April, 1937.

other nations to protect their own foreign trade. Among such measures have been competitive currency depreciation, tariff increases, imposition of quotas, embargoes, anti-dumping laws, sumptuary regulations, extreme sanitary regulations, exchange restrictions, blocked currencies, bilateral trade treaties, clearing agreements, rearmament policies, and the like. Also, on the side of increasing American foreign trade, the Administration's trade treaties should be given some of the credit. But they were not effected through monetary manipulation.

The broad conclusion as to the gold policy seems undeniable that none of the objectives sought was accomplished, at least not through gold adjustment and readjustment. True, price and economic recovery have occurred, but the influences responsible are some distance removed from gold manipulations.

A problem raised by increasing the price of gold, which overshadows whatever small benefits may have occurred, is seen in the phenomenal gold importations into the United States. In the four years beginning with February, 1934, net gold imports into the United States totaled well over $5,000,000,000. The situation was especially acute because of the excess-reserves situation. At the beginning of 1936, member banks of the Federal Reserve System reported $3,000,000,000 in excess reserves. By the end of that year, even after the 50 percent increase in required reserves on August 15, 1936, there was still a $2,000,000,000 excess.

One way in which the Treasury attempted to offset the growth in excess reserves, and of course in the enormous potentialities of credit inflation, was to "sterilize" gold purchases, from imports and from domestic mines. Instead of giving the Federal Reserve Banks gold certificates in exchange for gold, the Treasury in effect gave Treasury bills, and in this way refrained from building up the general bank-credit base. This procedure has turned out to be not without cost. In the year following the commencement of "sterilization," the Treasury reported more than $1,000,000,000 worth of gold in its "inactive fund." (See Chart III.) In other words, an increase in the interest-bearing debt took place for this purpose and to that amount. Even if the "inactive fund" should be maintained at only that amount, and not be increased any further,[2] and assuming the continuation of an interest rate equal to the average interest rate on outstanding debt (which at the end of December, 1937, amounted to 2.568 percent),[3] the Treasury would be paying out around $30,000,000 per year in order to "sterilize" gold. The average rate on bills, even though only between ½ and 1 percent, would entail an annual charge on the budget ranging from $5,000,000 to $10,000,000. The Treasury could avoid this dilemma to some extent by lowering its buying price for gold to less than $35.00 per ounce, and thus could discourage some of the gold import. Such a procedure would not affect the gold dollar, but would merely change the world price of gold as far as United States Treasury purchases were concerned. True, it would set up two separate categories for gold—open-market gold, and monetary gold. But that would be no different from the situation with respect to silver, which is in three separate categories—open-market, newly mined domestic, and "nationalized."

The gold policies of the Administration have failed signally to reach the goals set up, and have instead raised problems even more dangerous and difficult of solution. Instead of correcting the maldistribution of gold, they have aggravated it still more, and have made the United States an even greater dumping-ground for the world's needed gold. It still remains to be seen whether the United States will be burdened with the whole world's supply of precious metals—that is, whether other nations will decide to abandon gold (or silver) permanently as a monetary standard. Such an eventuality is unlikely, but nonetheless its possibility should not be too summarily dismissed.

APPRAISAL OF THE SILVER POLICY

The alleged purposes for the Government's undertaking of the silver policies were to raise prices and to restore foreign trade. As noted above, these same objectives were offered to justify the gold policy. They proved as difficult of accomplishment in the one case as in the other. As in the case of gold, the

[2] Cf. *supra*, p. 38.
[3] Including long-term Treasury Bonds, as well as Treasury Bills.

silver producer now gets a higher price for his product than he would in a free open market. Consequently the United States has become the sink not only for the world's gold, but also for its silver. Just how far this Midas-like policy can proceed is questionable. If all the rest of the world becomes dependent upon the United States for its monetary reserves, whether they consist of gold or of silver, it may decide to abandon the idea of any metallic base at all, and openly and frankly go over to a permanent, managed standard—a standard which could be so managed that the United States would find its gold and silver quite oppressive.

Although the steps taken on behalf of silver were allegedly for monetary purposes, their effects in that direction have been of little significance. True, the nation's currency has been watered by the inclusion of silver at a price almost three times its value in the open market. But that is not much worse than in the case of Federal Reserves notes, say, which are backed partly by over-valued gold and partly by Government securities which are redeemable in other types of paper only. In its monetary aspect, then, silver is just one of several "currency-dilution" items. However, the fact that the issuance of silver certificates has to date just about equaled the quantity of national bank notes retired,[4] is some apology, however small, for their issuance as a means of preventing a contraction of the circulating currency.

The really effective results of the silver policy were felt by the domestic miner and by foreign nations, the former to his benefit and the latter to their detriment. The Government's gift to the miner, and the financial disturbances imposed upon foreign nations, were fully discussed in the section on silver and need not be repeated here.[5]

The broad conclusion on the silver policy too is that none of the objectives sought was obtained. Instead, results developed which were not even thought of, much less mentioned, by the advocates of the policy. One result was, of course, the domestic subsidy to the silverites, a gift pure and simple. The

[4] As pointed out *supra*, p. 96.
[5] See *supra*, p. 77, *et seq*.

other was the disruption in the financial machinery of several friendly nations. While some partial relief might now be obtained through outright revocation and repeal of the silver policy, so much damage has been done already that even such relief would be late and of little help.

APPRAISAL OF THE OTHER MONETARY POLICIES: FEDERAL RESERVE NOTES

For Federal Reserve notes, the first changes occurred during the Hoover Administration with the passage, on February 27, 1932, of the Glass-Steagall amendment to the Federal Reserve Act. By permitting the substitution of Government obligations for gold, as collateral for Federal Reserve notes above the 40 percent minimum gold required, the first step toward currency manipulation was taken in this country in recent years. Whatever the merit of the amendment at the time of its passage, it is ineffective now. Because of the upward revaluation of gold, and as a result of the enormous gold influx, there is little need to use anything but gold as backing. Indeed, time and again in the recent past the gold coverage for the volume of notes as a whole topped 100 percent. (See Chart IX.) However, in order to be prepared for some future emergency, it might be just as well to keep the Glass-Steagall provision. But why not frankly make it a permanent part of the Federal Reserve Act, instead of extending it time and again as a temporary measure, now for one year, now for two?

It is deplorable, though, that a currency which was created to fluctuate with the ebbs and flows of business, as reflected in bills, acceptances, and other available eligible paper, has now potentially become but another national bank note which can be backed to a large extent (60 percent) by Government obligations instead. It may be argued that the fact that business concerns now finance themselves chiefly through the stock and investment markets, rather than obtain their financing from the commercial banks, spells the doom of commercial banking; and, consequently, that Federal Reserve notes with the attributes of an elastic currency, reflecting the needs of business and oscillating with those needs, have no vital function to perform in our modern monetary system. That question is beyond the scope of this study, but it does give rise to a whole series of questions whose answers would be helpful in appraising the Government's monetary policies of the past few years, both as to aims and as to future consequences.

If, perchance, the Glass-Steagall amendment should finally be allowed to expire in 1939, its present legal expiring date, then the Federal Reserve notes will return to their original status. The trend of thought in the present Administration's policy, however, seems weighted strongly against allowing the amendment to lapse. Current policy suggests, rather, a continuation of the process of pushing ahead the ultimate expiry date of this, as of other, monetary legislation.

FEDERAL RESERVE BANK NOTES

Federal Reserve bank notes are generally an emergency currency, and their issue was usually resorted to when other types of currency could not be obtained readily enough. There was little need for this particular type of currency, even in an emergency, and the earnest hope of most monetary economists is that these notes will be buried once and for all. Also, in view of the wide powers now available to issue Federal Reserve notes, the functions of these bank notes seem to have disappeared entirely.

NATIONAL BANK NOTES

When the bonds backing the national bank notes were called, it was stated that the procedure was being undertaken in order to "simplify" the currency. That may have been one of the reasons. Another probable reason was that by retiring these notes through using the remaining gold dollar devaluation "profit," the portion of the "profit" which was still free at that time, and which was a temptation to some of the inflationary-minded Congressmen, would be taken out of their reach, since it would be earmarked for the retirement of the national bank notes. With both these objectives, I believe, no economist can find fault.

National bank notes were useful for the first half-century or so of their existence after their establishment in 1863. Many disadvantages, however, became apparent by the early years of the new century. But the deathblow supposedly struck them by the Federal Reserve Act of December 23, 1913, required more than two decades to take effect. The need for these notes disappeared with the advent of Federal Reserve notes. In addition, the trend in the increased uses of deposit currency also obviated some of their functions, just as deposit currency may supplant other types of paper currency still in existence, except of course for small-change purposes.

UNITED STATES NOTES

If the Treasury was so intent upon simplification of the currency, it is somewhat surprising that it did not abolish the United States notes too. These notes are of small importance in any case, and no major change in policy would be necessary to get rid of them. It may be hoped, though, that in the not-too-distant future they too will be eliminated. Then the paper currency of the United States will consist of only two types—Federal Reserve notes and silver certificates.[6] It is too much to expect, of course, that silver certificates will ever be eliminated, leaving thus only one type of paper currency—Federal Reserve notes.

CONCLUSIONS

The monetary policies of the United States, on the whole, have failed to accomplish the objectives set for them. The gold policies increased our monetary troubles instead of lessening them. The silver policies reacted harmfully upon the rest of the world, and gave us no compensating benefits. Federal Reserve currency is no longer the reflector of business activity, expanding and contracting with trade as it was originally intended to do. True, its volume can vary according to demand, but that demand can arise from business activity, hoarding or any other cause, whether it elicit self-liquidating commercial paper or not.

Only as regards minor currency has anything of significance

[6] Gold certificates, in practice, serve only as asset items in the Federal Reserve Banks, for currency and deposit backing.

and benefit been accomplished. Bank notes, both national bank notes and Federal Reserve bank notes, seem definitely on the way to extinction—a very desirable process.

The present currency situation in the United States can be summed up as follows. We are on a so-called "streamlined" gold standard, that is, a gold standard which can go up, down, or sidewise with little, if any, friction. Such a gold standard is, in reality, a managed currency standard and not a gold standard at all. We are also on somewhat of a silver standard; that is, we accept all the newly mined domestic silver offered to the Treasury, purchase some silver in world markets, and issue silver certificates. This phase of the Administration's monetary policies, which could have been allowed to expire on December 31, 1937, was extended instead. It will thus continue to give our currency a surfeit of silver seasoning. We are also on a restricted bimetallic standard, with both gold and silver as part of our standard money.

The real fact of the matter is that we are on no fixed currency standard at all. Whatever the basis of our twenty-four-hour operations, it is not gold, nor silver, nor a combination of the two.

Our circulation is not an automatic, self-adjusting currency. As for its being a managed currency, we do not know upon what principles it is being managed. The nation's currency is indeed on a day-to-day basis with no definite, fixed objective, no commonly known standard of operation, and no underlying permanent policy.

PROPOSALS AND RECOMMENDATIONS

Now that we have reviewed the monetary policies of the United States Government for the period 1932 to 1938, it might be well to make a few recommendations as to future policy. Assuming the situation as it now is, and without hopeless wishing for a dead past, the question may be asked: Just what should be done to promote confidence in the currency and to prevent further watering?

First, of course, is the gold glut problem. It should now be possible to resume the full gold standard in international dealings. That is to say, gold should be permitted to move freely into and out of the nation, without penalty or need for license, pleas, affidavits, or other hindrances. It may be well to limit internal gold movements, but this should be done informally rather than by stringent legislation. I do not advocate return to the gold dollar of the pre-devaluation period, for on the one hand that would be asking for what is politically impossible; on the other hand, the fact that, after four years, the business system has more or less adjusted itself to the new currency, makes a reversion economically undesirable as well.

The President's power to change the weight of the gold dollar should not be extended when it expires on June 30, 1939. The dollar ought permanently to be left at its present weight. The exchange stabilization fund should not be given another lease on life after its expiry, also on June 30, 1939. International commercial and financial relationships should be determined by the businessmen themselves, and should not be dependent upon governmental whim.

Repeal of the Silver Purchase Act is desirable. Subsidies to non-essential industries, as silver mining, should be abolished, even under the guise of monetary policy. Agreements which the United States has with China, Mexico, and Canada, to exchange gold or dollar balances for silver, are unnecessary, and, with repeal of the Silver Purchase Act, should be allowed to lapse. Although it has been asserted that these international monetary relationships are free from political implications, such repercussions are entirely within the realm of dangerous possibility.[7]

The Glass-Steagall amendment to the Federal Reserve Act either should be repealed or should be made a permanent section of the Act. Although it is not an indispensable section of that Act, it will, for the most part, be more or less innocuous, so that it might just as well be left a part of the law as removed. It might possibly serve to bolster confidence, during some future emergency.

[7] Witness the effects of the March 28, 1938, announcement, by the United States Treasury Department, of the suspension of silver purchases from the Mexican Government.

Federal Reserve bank notes should be retired, never to be reissued again. There is now no need for them, and if the Glass-Steagall amendment becomes a permanent part of the Federal Reserve Act, whatever functions these bank notes could conceivably have can be assumed by Federal Reserve notes.

The Government should use the silver seigniorage already acquired to retire the "Greenbacks," just as it used the gold dollar devaluation "profit" to retire national bank notes. In a sense, gold dollar devaluation "profit" and silver seigniorage are identical. They both result from a difference between present monetary value of the respective monetary metal and either a previous monetary value, or the open-market or other price, such as Government "nationalization" or other purchase price. Also, in line with the retirement of the existing "Greenbacks," the provision in the "Thomas" Amendment permitting further issue of fiat currency should be definitely and unequivocally repealed.

To sum up then: first, the United States should return to an international gold standard; secondly, silver dilution of the currency ought to be brought to an end; and finally, "Greenbacks" should be retired, and the right to issue them in the future revoked.

APPENDIX A

CHRONOLOGIES

ALTHOUGH this book is concerned mainly with monetary policies of 1932 to 1937, it was thought advisable, for purposes of background and perspective, as well as for convenient reference, to include in the chronologies all the important events in this field since the establishment of the United States as a nation.

Even though the chronologies are presented in three parts—Gold, Silver, Miscellaneous—individual items under each part are sometimes applicable to other parts also. An airtight separation is of necessity impossible, but an attempt is made to place each item where most relevant, and if of large enough significance, to place it under more than one heading.

1. CHRONOLOGY OF IMPORTANT EVENTS RELATING TO GOLD

1792 April 2 — United States Mint established
Monetary system of the United States created
Gold dollar to contain 24.75 grains of pure gold, silver dollar to contain 371.25 grains of pure silver. Ratio, therefore, 15 to 1

1834 June 28 — Revision of money standard reduces amount of gold in dollar by 6.26 percent
Gold dollar set at 25.8 grains, or 23.2 grains of fine gold (Fineness, therefore, 0.899225)
Ratio becomes 16.002+ to 1

1837 January 18 — Act to make fineness of gold and silver coins uniform
Gold dollar fixed at 25.8 grains of gold, 0.900 fine, therefore, 23.22 grains of pure gold, making devaluation of 1792 gold dollar, 6.18 percent
Ratio 15.988+ to 1

1848 January — Gold discovered in California

1873 February 12 — Silver demonetized, when gold dollar made the unit of value of the United States, and silver to be legal tender up to $5.00 only

1875 January 14 — Act provides for resumption of specie payments on January 1, 1879

1879 January 1 — Resumption of specie payments effective

1896 — Gold the victor in Free Silver campaign

1900 March 14 — Passage of Gold Standard Act, declaring that the dollar, containing 25.8 grains of gold 0.900 fine, "shall be the standard unit of

117

value," and the Secretary of the Treasury is to maintain all forms of United States money at a parity with this standard

1917 August 27	Embargo on gold exports
1917 October 6	Trading-with-the-Enemy Act
1919 June 26	Removal of gold export embargo
1919 December 24	Gold certificates declared unlimited legal tender
1925 April 28	England resumes gold standard
1931 September 21	England abandons gold standard
1932 February 27	Glass-Steagall Act signed. Permits substitution of United States Treasury obligations for gold, as Federal Reserve note backing above the 40 percent minimum gold reserve required, when sufficient eligible paper is not available
1933 February 3	Hoover signs bill extending Glass-Steagall Amendment for 1 year
1933 March 6	Presidential Bank Holiday Proclamation which, among other provisions, places an export embargo on gold, and prohibits banks from paying out gold
1933 March 7	Permission granted for export of earmarked gold
1933 March 8	Federal Reserve Board requests from Federal Reserve Banks names of all persons who withdrew gold from Federal Reserve Banks or member banks since February 1, 1933
1933 March 9	Emergency Banking Act signed, confirming and extending March 6 Proclamation, and granting the President emergency powers over foreign exchange, gold and currency move-. ments, and banking transactions
1933 April 5	Executive order "nationalizes" gold by forbidding the hoarding of gold, and requiring that all gold be delivered to the Federal Reserve Banks, directly or through the member banks, who were to deliver their gold also
1933 April 13	License for export of $600,000 gold to Holland —first export since proclamation of bank holiday
1933 April 18	Issuance of licenses for gold export discontinued

1933 April 19	Secretary of Treasury advises that "no further licenses would be granted for export of gold from the United States for the purpose of supporting the dollar in foreign exchange"
1933 April 20	Gold Embargo.—Executive order prohibits earmarking of gold for foreign account, or export of gold coin, bullion or certificates, except that gold already earmarked for foreign governments or central banks, and for the Bank for International Settlements, or needed for the fulfillment of contracts entered into prior to April 5, 1933, could be exported in the discretion of the Secretary of the Treasury
1933 April 20	"Thomas" (Inflation) Amendment to Agricultural Adjustment Act offered in Congress
1933 May 1	Presidential executive order issued subjecting gold hoarding to penalties
1933 May 6	Resolution abrogating gold clause introduced in Congress
1933 May 7	During "fireside chat," President states that as there is not enough gold to pay all holders of gold obligations, "in the interest of justice" none should be paid
	He states, also, that forthcoming London Economic Conference "must succeed . . . we have each of us pledged ourselves to the best joint efforts to that end"
1933 May 12	"Thomas" Amendment passed. Permits 50 percent gold dollar devaluation
1933 May 16	President, in message to nations participating in forthcoming Economic Conference, says: "The conference must establish order in place of the present chaos by a stabilization of currencies, by freeing the flow of world trade, and by international action to raise price levels"
1933 June 5	Gold clause abrogated in all public and private contracts, past and future
	All forms of United States currency made legal tender
1933 July 3	President Roosevelt's message to London Economic Conference rejecting monetary program proposed by gold bloc

1933 July 8	Gold bloc countries of Europe declare adherence to gold standard
1933 August 29	Export of newly mined gold authorized under Treasury regulations
	Anti-hoarding order made more stringent
1933 September 8	Treasury announces first sales of newly mined gold for export through Federal Reserve Banks, with price at $29.62
1933 September 13	First shipment abroad of newly mined gold
1933 October 22	In radio address, President announces policy of raising commodity prices, hence to establish a Government market for gold, and to move toward a managed currency
1933 October 25	Executive order authorizes Reconstruction Finance Corporation to purchase newly mined domestic gold
1933 October 29	President announces plans for Reconstruction Finance Corporation to purchase gold abroad
1933 December 28	Executive order requires delivery of all gold coin (except rare coin), gold bullion and gold certificates to the Treasurer of the United States
1934 January 15	Secretary of Treasury sets January 17 as expiration date for surrender of gold under December 28, 1933 order
	President Roosevelt sends Gold message to Congress
1934 January 30	Passage of Gold Reserve Act
1934 January 31	Presidential proclamation devalues gold dollar to 59.06 percent of former weight, thus raising price of gold from $20.67 to $35.00 per fine ounce, i. e., cuts weight from 25.8 to $15\frac{5}{21}$ grains of gold, 0.900 fine
1934 March 6	President Roosevelt signs bill extending Glass-Steagall amendment to March 3, 1935, or, in his discretion, to March 3, 1937
1934 April 27	Exchange stabilization fund first set up as separate item in published Treasury statements
1934 November 12	Restrictions on foreign-exchange transactions and exports of currency liberalized, by replacing specific license requirements with a general license

1935 January 8–11   Gold-clause abrogation cases argued before the United States Supreme Court

1935 January 15   United States Treasury intervenes to stabilize foreign exchange

1935 February 11   Secretary of Treasury promises use of stabilization fund to keep dollar steady, as he had been doing for previous month

1935 February 14   Proclamation by the President, extending Glass-Steagall provisions for substitution of Governments as collateral for Federal Reserve notes, to March 3, 1937

1935 February 18   United States Supreme Court upholds constitutionality of gold clause abrogation

1935 March 20   United States Treasury sells 32,000 ounces of gold to Mexico in exchange for silver

1935 March 21   Secretary of Treasury states willingness to consider applications by other nations wishing to buy gold from the United States

1935 March 25   Ambassador Bingham, in press interview in London, urges currency stabilization "when the proper time comes"

1935 April 3   United States Treasury announces sale of more gold to Bank of Mexico to increase reserves, amounting to 51,300 ounces valued at $1,800,000

1935 April 8   United States Treasury announces sale of 86,000 ounces of gold to Venezuela and 30,000 ounces more to Mexico in exchange for silver

1935 May 13   Secretary of Treasury defends United States gold policy and states willingness to stabilize, but not on terms disadvantageous to the United States

1935 June 16   President Tannery of Bank of France discloses part played by United States in recent franc crisis

1935 June 27   Presidential message asks Congress to outlaw damage suits based on gold-clause abrogation

1935 August 23   Banking Act of 1935 becomes law. Among other things, it gives Board of Governors of the Federal Reserve System authority to double the then-existing reserve requirements

1935 August 27 Gold-Clause Act becomes law:
(1) Holders of gold-clause securities of the United States may redeem such securities until July 1, 1936
(2) Government may no longer be sued on account of such gold-clause securities, coin or currency or gold or silver seizure

1936 January 10 Presidential proclamation extends power to vary weight of gold dollar, and life of stabilization fund, for one year, or until January 30, 1937

1936 February 3 New York bank gets license to ship $5,000,000 in gold to France and Holland. This was the first export since October 1934

1936 February 8 Additional gold exports of $3,935,000 to Europe

1936 July 14 Board of Governors of the Federal Reserve System announces 50 percent increase in reserve requirements, effective August 15

1936 September 22 League of Nations Financial Committee recommends that France, the Netherlands and Switzerland "readjust" their currencies to the pound and the dollar

1936 September 25 Federal Reserve Bank of New York announces $43,532,000 gold engaged in Paris, bringing total since beginning of August to $197,700,000

1936 September 25 Secretary of Treasury announces tripartite agreement between United States, France, and Great Britain for coöperative stabilization of each nation's currency and for maintenance of equilibrium in international exchange (Agreement conditional on devaluation of the franc)

1936 September 26 Poland announces it will not devalue its currency despite France's action, but stands ready to join the tripartite agreement

1936 September 26 United States purchases £1,000,000 offered by Russia, with $5,000,000 from stabilization fund, to protect an alleged attack against the tripartite agreement

1936 September 28 Netherlands temporarily abandons gold standard, and creates a stabilization fund, but does not fix a definite value for the guilder

1936 September 30 Swiss franc authorized to be devalued by 26 to 34 percent

1936 October 1   Devaluation of French franc by 29 percent becomes effective

1936 October 5   Italy devalues currency (and reduces import tariffs)

1936 October 12   Secretary of Treasury announces that United States, Great Britain, and France have concluded a reciprocal agreement providing for purchase and sale of gold through their stabilization funds, in order to stabilize the pound, the dollar and the franc. Plan is said to be on a twenty-four-hour basis

1936 November 23 Secretary of Treasury announces that Belgium, Switzerland and the Netherlands have joined in the September 25, 1936, tripartite agreement to promote international monetary equilibrium (Belgium, on September 26, had already informed the United States of its intention to adhere to the principles of the agreement)

1936 November 23 Secretary of Treasury abolishes private gold exports, stating that gold is to move only through the exchange stabilization fund

1936 December 21 Treasury announces new policy of "sterilizing" newly mined or imported gold, in order to prevent it from increasing excess reserves

1936 December 24 Treasury Daily Statement shows, for first time, amount of "sterilized" or "inactive" gold— $14,835,000

1937 January 23   Law signed extending until June 30, 1939, the life of the exchange stabilization fund, and the President's power to vary the weight of the gold dollar

1937 January 30   Board of Governors of the Federal Reserve System announces increase of $33\frac{1}{3}$ percent in required reserves, thus doubling reserve requirements in force when the Banking Act of 1935 was passed. Half of the increase is to take effect on March 1, and the rest on May 1

1937 March 1   Law signed extending authority to issue Federal Reserve notes against Government securities until June 30, 1939 (Glass-Steagall Act)

1937 March 4	Excess reserves of member banks drop $790,000,000, following upon March 1 increase in reserve requirements
1937 May 1	Effective date of increased reserve requirements, resulting in a doubling of the requirements in effect prior to passage of the Banking Act of 1935
1937 May 19	Bank of England purchase of $21,409,000 worth of gold as part of alleged plan to lighten burden on United States
1937 May 20	Secretary of Treasury states his opposition to any general monetary conference, but favors individual parleys
1937 June 1	Secretary of Treasury states that tripartite agreement has stabilized foreign exchange; also, he denies rumor that the Treasury is planning to reduce its gold-buying price
1937 June 29	France states she may be forced to withdraw from the tripartite agreement
1937 June 30	French Cabinet Council modifies monetary law of October 1, 1936, by removing gold-content limitations set at that time
1937 July 1	Statement issued by United States Secretary of Treasury to effect that an understanding has been reached with France and Great Britain for continuation of the tripartite agreement
1937 July 9	United States again agrees to sell gold to China, in exchange for Chinese silver; gold is to remain in the United States, however
1937 July 15	United States agrees to make $6,000,000 gold available to Brazil to aid stability of the milreis
1937 August 18	Acting Secretary of Treasury states willingness of United States to aid in "stability" of international currencies, but does not favor "rigid" stabilization
1937 September 12	Board of Governors of the Federal Reserve System announces release by Treasury of $300,000,000 of "sterilized" gold to ease seasonal credit demands
1937 November 8	Gold ($10,250,000) from "inactive" fund engaged for shipment to France—first major export of gold in several years

1937 November 10 Treasury announces $5,000,000 gold from "inactive" fund to be shipped to England for British stabilization account

1937 November 18 Federal Reserve System announces $18,000,000 increase in holdings of Governments over past week

1938 February 14 Secretary of Treasury announces modification in gold "sterilization" policy. Retroactively to January 1, 1938, "sterilization" will be applied only to that amount of gold received each quarter which is in excess of $100,000,000

1938 April 14 Treasury "desterilizes" all gold in "inactive" fund

1938 April 16 Board of Governors of the Federal Reserve System announces decrease of 12½ percent in required reserves

1938 April 18 Treasury announces discontinuance of "sterilization" policy

2. CHRONOLOGY OF IMPORTANT EVENTS RELATING TO SILVER

1786   Congress of the Confederation establishes as the monetary unit the silver dollar of 375.64 grains of pure silver (never coined)

1792 April 2   United States Mint established
Monetary system of the United States created Gold dollar to contain 24.75 grains of pure gold, silver dollar to contain 371.25 grains of pure silver; ratio, therefore, 15 to 1

1837 January 18   Act to make fineness of gold and silver coins uniform. Gold dollar fixed at 25.8 grains of gold, 0.900 fine, therefore 23.22 grains of pure gold, making devaluation of 1792 gold dollar, 6.18 percent. Ratio 15.988+ to 1

1853 February 21   Silver coins of denomination less than $1.00 deweighted by 6½ percent. A half dollar to contain 192.9 grains, 0.900 fine, or 173.6 grains of pure silver, but the dollar unchanged at 412.5 and 371.3 grains, respectively
Likewise, other fractional silver devalued by 6½ percent. Legal tender up to $5.00, only

1873 February 12   Silver demonetized, when gold dollar made the unit of value of the United States, and silver to be legal tender up to $5.00 only

1878 February 28   Bland-Allison Act:
(1) Reinstates silver as legal tender for all contracts unless specifically stated otherwise
(2) Secretary of Treasury to purchase silver bullion, at market price, not less than $2,000,000 worth nor more than $4,000,000 worth per month, and to coin it into silver dollars

1890 July 14   Passage of Sherman Silver Purchase Act. Secretary of Treasury to purchase 4,500,000 ounces of silver bullion per month, at the market price, but not exceeding $1 for 371.25 grains of pure silver, and to issue United States Treasury notes in payment. Also, 2,000,000 ounces to be coined each

126

month until July 1, 1891, and thereafter as much as necessary to redeem these Treasury notes

1892 November 1   Repeal of Sherman Silver Purchase Act

1918 April 23   Pittman Act passed providing for melting down of silver dollars, and converting into bullion (over 270,000,000 silver dollars were converted, and later recoined)

1933 May 12   "Thomas" Amendment

Silver may be fixed in any ratio to gold, whenever the President finds such action necessary to stabilize domestic prices or to protect foreign commerce of United States against adverse effect of depreciated foreign currencies

Silver (as all other coin and currency) made legal tender

Silver may be received, to a limited extent, for payment on foreign Government debts, during next 6 months

1933 June 15   Great Britain, Italy, and some others make token payment, in silver, on war-debt account

Finland pays full installment

France *et als.* default

1933 July 22   London Silver Agreement signed. Leading producing nations to buy and hold domestic silver. Leading users not to debase coinage, demonetize silver, or dispose of silver in any way

1933 December 21   Executive order provides for purchase of newly mined domestic silver at 64.64 cents per fine ounce, thus, in effect, ratifying silver agreement of July 22, 1933

1934 May 22   President Roosevelt sends Silver Message to Congress

1934 June 19   Passage of Silver Purchase Act

1934 June 28   Export of silver forbidden except under license

1934 August 9   Silver "nationalized"

1934 August 19–
October 12   Exchange of notes—United States and China— as regards detrimental effects on China of United States silver policy

1934 October 3   China protests officially to United States

1934 October 14–15	China increases export duty on silver, and adds on an equalization charge
1935 January 4	Senator Wheeler introduces bill for free coinage of silver, 16 to 1 (Not passed)
1935 March 20	United States Treasury sells 32,000 ounces of gold to Mexico in exchange for silver
1935 April 10	Executive order of December 21, 1933, amended by increasing price of newly mined domestic silver from 64.64 to 71.11 cents per fine ounce (World price, 64 cents)
1935 April 24	Executive order of December 21, 1933, again amended by increasing price of newly mined domestic silver from 71.11 to 77.57 cents per fine ounce (World price, $71\frac{5}{8}$ cents)
1935 April 25	Mexico calls in silver coins, prohibits export of silver
1935 April 27	Mexico, in order to adjust monetary system, declares bank holiday, orders all silver coins to be exchanged for paper notes, prohibits export of silver coin
1935 May 3	Peru places export embargo on silver bars and coins, and prohibits hoarding, buying, or selling of silver
1935 May 12	Dr. H. H. Kung, Chinese Minister of Finance, attributes credit and currency contraction in China to United States silver policies
1935 May 17	Ecuador places embargo on silver exports
1935 May 20	Import embargo, by United States, on foreign silver coins or forms of silver used as money, whose monetary value is less than 110 percent of open-market value of its silver content
1935 May 21	Ecuador issues notes to relieve scarcity of silver coins which are being hoarded
1935 July 9	United States Government uses exchange equalization fund to purchase 15,000,000 ounces of silver in London, to avert collapse on heavy selling from India and China
1935 August 13	Heavy silver selling by Far East breaks United States peg
1935 November 1	Chinese exchange breaks badly
1935 November 3	China abandons silver in favor of a managed standard, "nationalizes" silver, and pegs exchange rate

1935 November 9	Hong Kong places export embargo on silver
1935 December 11	No market price quoted for silver in London—first time since 1914—as result of temporary halt in purchasing by United States Treasury
1935 December 13	Manchukuo abandons silver
1935 December 31	Silver talks are begun between Secretary Morgenthau and the Mexican Secretary of the Treasury Suarez
1936 January 6	Silver agreement reached between United States and Mexico
1936 January 24	President Roosevelt denies silver revaluation rumors
1936 February 5	For first time in two months London silver market resumes forward operations
1936 March 4	Secretary of Treasury authorizes Federal Reserve Bank of New York to purchase, through Bank of Canada, newly mined Canadian silver in such amounts as to be fixed each month
1936 March 5	Treasury indicates it may purchase all of newly mined silver of South American countries
1936 May 18	Secretary of Treasury announces agreement between the United States and China, for currency-stabilization purposes, whereby United States Treasury will purchase silver from the Central Bank of China with gold
1936 July 1	Bank of China formally opens New York agency; first time that a leading Chinese bank has directly entered the American financial field. Aim is to promote trade between the United States and China
1936 August 31	President Cardenas of Mexico decrees resumption of silver coinage on September 1
1937 January 11	United States Supreme Court upholds silver tax on profits made while Silver Purchase Act of 1934 was pending
1937 February 11	United States earmarks $9,970,400 for Bank of China, to pay for silver
1937 July 9	United States again agrees to sell gold to China, in exchange for Chinese silver; gold is to remain in the United States, however
1937 September 15	Treasury announces continuation, after the expiry date of December 31, 1937, of purchases of newly mined domestic silver

1937 December 30   Purchase of silver from Canada, Mexico, and China is to be continued, on a month-to-month basis, through at least July 1, 1938

1937 December 31   President issues proclamation to continue purchases of newly mined domestic silver, but reducing price from 77.57 cents per fine ounce to 64.64 cents

1938 March 28   United States Treasury announces suspension of silver purchases from Mexican Government

3. CHRONOLOGY OF IMPORTANT EVENTS RELATING TO OTHER COINS AND CURRENCY, ETC.

(a) Bank Notes (National Bank Notes and Federal Reserve Bank Notes)

1864 June 3	Act provides for issuance of national bank notes (originally provided for by Act of February 25, 1863, which was repealed and superseded by this Act)
1932 July 22	Rider to Federal Home Loan Bank Act extends "circulation privilege" to all United States bonds with coupon rate not exceeding $3\frac{3}{8}$ percent
1933 March 9	Emergency Banking Act permits issuance of Federal Reserve bank notes, with wide latitude as to collateral
1935 March 9, 11	Treasury announcement and call for redemption of 2 percent bonds bearing circulation privilege, the Consols of 1930 on July 1 and the 2 percent Panama Canal loans on August 1. Redemption, for the most part, will be from the $642,000,000 remaining devaluation "profit"
1935 March 28	Completion of retirement of Federal Reserve bank notes issued under Emergency Banking Act of March 9, 1933
1935 July 1	Call date of 2 percent Consols of 1930, heretofore kept outstanding because of their "circulation privilege"
1935 July 22	"Circulation privilege" expires for United States bonds bearing interest rate of $3\frac{3}{8}$ percent or less (see item for July 22, 1932)
1935 August 1	Call date of 2 percent Panama Canal bonds, heretofore kept outstanding because of their "circulation privilege"

131

(b) "Greenbacks"

1861 July 17, August 5	First paper money ever issued by the Government of the United States—"Demand notes," payable on demand at certain designated subtreasuries
1862 February 25	Substitution of United States notes ("Greenbacks") in place of demand notes Total amount authorized by various Acts, $450,000,000, of which $50,000,000 was to be but a temporary issue Highest amount outstanding (January 30, 1864), $449,338,902
1862 March 17	Greenbacks made legal tender First use of term "lawful money"
1866 April 12	United States notes to be retired by $10,000,000 during next six months, and $4,000,000 a month thereafter. Of $70,000,000 authorized to be retired, only $44,000,000 was actually retired, leaving outstanding $356,000,000 of the "permanent" issue
1867	Contraction of greenback currency
1868 February 4	Act of April 12, 1866 repealed
1873 June 20	Outstanding amount of United States notes fixed at $382,000,000
1875 January 14	Act provides for reduction of United States notes to $300,000,000
1878 May 31	Act requires reissuance of United States notes when redeemed. The $346,681,016 then outstanding continues to the present (1938)

(c) Banking Holiday of 1933

1933 February 14	8-day banking moratorium declared in Michigan
1933 February 24	3-day banking moratorium declared in Maryland
1933 March 2–4	Increasing number of States declare bank holidays, and by March 4 practically all banks in country are closed or operating under restrictions
1933 March 6	President proclaims 4-day nation-wide bank holiday
1933 March 9	President issues proclamation extending banking holiday indefinitely (still in effect at end of 1937)
1933 March 13–15	Re-opening of banks: on March 13th, those in Federal Reserve Bank cities on March 14th, those in clearing-house cities on March 15th, elsewhere

(d) Miscellaneous

1792	February 25	Bank of the United States incorporated
1811	March	Closing of United States Bank
1816	April 10	Second Bank of the United States incorporated
1817	January	Second United States Bank opened
1818	August	United States Bank suspends specie payments
1832	July	President Jackson vetoes renewal of United States Bank charter
1836	March	Charter of United States Bank expires (Pennsylvania charter obtained)
1837		General suspension of specie payments
1857	October–December	Specie payments suspended
1860	November	Issuance of clearing-house certificates
1861		Banks suspend specie payments
1863	February 25	National Bank Act passed
1865	March 3	Law passed imposing ten percent tax on State bank circulation, effective July 1, 1866
1869	September 24	Black Friday panic, gold corner
1873	September–November	Banks suspend currency payments
1908	May 30	Aldrich-Vreeland Emergency Currency Act becomes law. Provides for "National Currency Association" to issue emergency notes collateralled by municipal and railroad bonds, and commercial paper (In effect, a legalization of clearing-house certificates)
1911	January	Senator Aldrich proposes a "Reserve Association"
1913	December 23	Passage of Federal Reserve Act. Provisions for issue of Federal Reserve notes, and Federal Reserve bank notes
1914	August 3	Clearing-house loan certificates issued, but retired within about three months
1914	August 5	Aldrich-Vreeland emergency currency issued
1933	June 12	Opening of London Monetary and Economic Conference
1933	July 27	Adjournment of London Conference
1937	April 29	Federal Reserve statement shows larger holdings of United States securities in preparation for that portion of the increase in reserve requirements effective May 1
1937	September 26	Board of Governors of the Federal Reserve System liberalizes eligibility requirements

APPENDIX B

REPRINTS OF LAWS, PORTIONS OF LAWS, ETC.

1. GLASS-STEAGALL ACT, SECTION 3

SEC. 3. The second paragraph of section 16 of the Federal Reserve Act, as amended, is amended to read as follows:

"Any Federal reserve bank may make application to the local Federal reserve agent for such amount of the Federal reserve notes hereinbefore provided for as it may require. Such application shall be accompanied with a tender to the local Federal reserve agent of collateral in amount equal to the sum of the Federal reserve notes thus applied for and issued pursuant to such application. The collateral security thus offered shall be notes, drafts, bills of exchange, or acceptances acquired under the provisions of section 13 of this Act, or bills of exchange indorsed by a member bank of any Federal reserve district and purchased under the provisions of section 14 of this Act, or bankers' acceptances purchased under the provisions of said section 14, or gold or gold certificates: *Provided, however,* That until March 3, 1933, should the Federal Reserve Board deem it in the public interest, it may, upon the affirmative vote of not less than a majority of its members, authorize the Federal reserve banks to offer, and the Federal reserve agents to accept, as such collateral security, direct obligations of the United States. On March 3, 1933, or sooner should the Federal Reserve Board so decide, such authorization shall terminate and such obligations of the United States be retired as security for Federal reserve notes. In no event shall such collateral security be less than the amount of Federal reserve notes applied for. The Federal reserve agent shall each day notify the Federal Reserve Board of all issues and withdrawals of Federal reserve notes to and by the Federal reserve bank to which he is accredited. The said Federal Reserve Board may at any time call upon a Federal reserve bank for additional security to protect the Federal reserve notes issued to it."

Approved, February 27, 1932

2. FEDERAL HOME LOAN BANK ACT, SEC. 29

SEC. 29. That notwithstanding any provisions of law prohibiting bonds of the United States from bearing the circulation privilege, for a period of three years from the date of enactment of this Act all outstanding bonds of the United States heretofore issued or issued during such period, bearing interest at a rate not exceeding $3\frac{3}{8}$ per centum per annum, shall be receivable by the Treasurer of the United States as security for the issuance of circulating notes to national banking associations, and upon the deposit with the Treasurer of the United States by a national banking association of any such bonds, such association shall be entitled to receive circulating notes in the same manner and to the same extent and subject to the same conditions and limitations now provided by law in the case of 2 per centum gold bonds of the United States bearing the circulation privilege; except that the limitation contained in section 9 of the Act of July 12, 1882, as amended, with respect to the amount of lawful money which may be deposited with the Treasurer of the United States by national banking associations for the purpose of withdrawing bonds held as security for their circulating notes, shall not apply to the bonds of the United States to which the circulation privilege is extended by this section and which are held as security for such notes. Nothing contained in this section shall be construed to modify, amend, or repeal any law relating to bonds of the United States which now bear the circulation privilege.

As used in this section, the word "bonds" shall not include notes, certificates, or bills issued by the United States.

There are hereby authorized to be appropriated such sums as may be necessary to carry out the provisions of this section.

Approved, July 22, 1932

3. EMERGENCY BANK ACT, TITLES I AND IV
AN ACT

To provide relief in the existing national emergency in banking, and for other purposes.

Be it enacted by the Senate and House of Representatives of the United States of America in Congress assembled, That the Congress hereby declares that a serious emergency exists and that it is imperatively necessary speedily to put into effect remedies of uniform national application.

TITLE I

SECTION 1. The actions, regulations, rules, licenses, orders and proclamations heretofore or hereafter taken, promulgated, made, or issued by the President of the United States or the Secretary of the Treasury since March 4, 1933, pursuant to the authority conferred by subdivision (b) of section 5 of the Act of October 6, 1917, as amended, are hereby approved and confirmed.

SEC. 2. Subdivision (b) of section 5 of the Act of October 6, 1917 (40 Stat. L. 411), as amended, is hereby amended to read as follows:

"(b) During time of war or during any other period of national emergency declared by the President, the President may, through any agency that he may designate, or otherwise, investigate, regulate, or prohibit, under such rules and regulations as he may prescribe, by means of licenses or otherwise, any transactions in foreign exchange, transfers of credit between or payments by banking institutions as defined by the President, and export, hoarding, melting, or earmarking of gold or silver coin or bullion or currency, by any person within the United States or any place subject to the jurisdiction thereof; and the President may require any person engaged in any transaction referred to in this subdivision to furnish under oath, complete information relative thereto, including the production of any books of account, contracts, letters or other papers, in connection therewith in the custody or control of such person, either before or after such transaction is completed. Whoever willfully violates any of the provisions of this subdivision or of any license, order, rule or regulation issued thereunder, shall, upon conviction, be fined not more than $10,000, or, if a natural person, may be imprisoned for not more than ten years, or both; and any officer, director, or agent of any corporation who knowingly participates in such violation may be punished by a like fine, imprisonment, or both. As used in this subdivision the term 'person' means an individual, partnership, association, or corporation."

SEC. 3. Section 11 of the Federal Reserve Act is amended by adding at the end thereof the following new subsection:

"(n) Whenever in the judgment of the Secretary of the Treasury such action is necessary to protect the currency system of the United States, the Secretary of the Treasury, in his discretion, may require any or all individuals, partnerships, associations and corporations to pay and deliver to the Treasurer of the United States any or all gold coin, gold bullion, and gold certificates owned by such individuals, partnerships, associations and corporations. Upon receipt of such gold coin, gold bullion or gold certificates, the Secretary of the Treasury shall pay therefor an equivalent amount of any other form of coin or currency coined or issued under the laws of the United States. The Secretary of the Treasury shall pay all costs of the transportation of such gold bullion, gold certificates, coin, or currency, including the cost of insurance, protection, and such other incidental costs as may be reasonably necessary. Any individual, partnership, association, or corporation failing to comply with any requirement of the Secretary of the Treasury made under this subsection shall be subject to a penalty equal to twice the value of the gold or gold certificates in respect of which such failure occurred, and such penalty may be collected by the Secretary of the Treasury by suit or otherwise."

SEC. 4. In order to provide for the safer and more effective operation of the National Banking System and the Federal Reserve System, to preserve for the people the full benefits of the currency provided for by the Congress through the National Banking System and the Federal Reserve System, and to relieve interstate commerce of the burdens and obstructions resulting from the receipt on an unsound or unsafe basis of deposits subject to withdrawal by check, during such emergency period as the President of the United States by proclamation may prescribe, no member bank of the Federal Reserve System shall transact any banking business except to such extent and subject to such regulations, limitations and restrictions as may be prescribed by the Secretary of the Treasury, with the approval of the President. Any individual, partnership, corporation, or association, or any director, officer or employee thereof, violating any of the provisions of this section shall be deemed guilty of a misdemeanor and, upon conviction thereof, shall be fined not more than $10,000 or, if a natural person, may, in addition to such fine, be imprisoned for a term not exceeding ten years. Each day that any such violation continues shall be deemed a separate offense.

TITLE IV

Sec. 401. The sixth paragraph of Section 18 of the Federal Reserve Act is amended to read as follows:

"Upon the deposit with the Treasurer of the United States, (a) of any direct obligations of the United States or (b) of any notes, drafts, bills of exchange, or bankers' acceptances acquired under the provisions of this Act, any Federal reserve bank making such deposit in the manner prescribed by the Secretary of the Treasury shall be entitled to receive from the Comptroller of the Currency circulating notes in blank, duly registered and countersigned. When such circulating notes are issued against the security of obligations of the United States, the amount of such circulating notes shall be equal to the face value of the direct obligations of the United States so deposited as security; and, when issued against the security of notes, drafts, bills of exchange and bankers' acceptances acquired under the provisions of this Act, the amount thereof shall be equal to not more than 90 per cent of the estimated value of such notes, drafts, bills of exchange and bankers' acceptances so deposited as security. Such notes shall be the obligations of the Federal reserve bank procuring the same, shall be in form prescribed by the Secretary of the Treasury, shall be receivable at par in all parts of the United States for the same purposes as are national bank notes, and shall be redeemable in lawful money of the United States on presentation at the United States Treasury or at the bank of issue. The Secretary of the Treasury is authorized and empowered to prescribe regulations governing the issuance, redemption, replacement, retirement and destruction of such circulating notes and the release and substitution of security therefor. Such circulating notes shall be subject to the same tax as is provided by law for the circulating notes of national banks secured by 2 per cent bonds of the United States. No such circulating notes shall be issued under this paragraph after the President has declared by proclamation that the emergency recognized by the President by proclamation of March 6, 1933, has terminated, unless such circulating notes are secured by deposits of bonds of the United States bearing the circulation privilege. When required to do so by the Secretary of the Treasury, each Federal reserve agent shall act as agent of the Treasurer of the United States or of the Comptroller of the Currency, or both, for the performance of any of the functions which the Treasurer or the Comptroller may be called upon to perform in carrying out the provisions of this paragraph. Appropriations available for distinctive paper and printing United States currency or national bank currency are hereby made available for the production of the circulating notes of Federal reserve banks herein provided; but the United States shall be reimbursed by the Federal reserve bank to which such notes are issued for all expenses necessarily incurred in connection with the procuring of such notes and all other expenses incidental to their issue, redemption, replacement, retirement and destruction."

SEC. 402. Section 10 (b) of the Federal Reserve Act, as amended, is further amended to read as follows:

"SEC. 10 (b). In exceptional and exigent circumstances, and when any member bank has no further eligible and acceptable assets available to enable it to obtain adequate credit accommodations through rediscounting at the Federal reserve bank or any other method provided by this Act other than that provided by section 10 (a), any Federal reserve bank, under rules and regulations prescribed by the Federal Reserve Board, may make advances to such member bank on its time or demand notes secured to the satisfaction of such Federal reserve bank. Each such note shall bear interest at a rate not less than 1 per centum per annum higher than the highest discount rate in effect at such Federal reserve bank on the date of such note. No advance shall be made under this section after March 3, 1934, or after the expiration of such additional period not exceeding one year as the President may prescribe."

SEC. 403. Section 13 of the Federal Reserve Act, as amended, is amended by adding at the end thereof the following new paragraph:

"Subject to such limitations, restrictions and regulations as the Federal Reserve Board may prescribe, any Federal reserve bank may make advances to any individual, partnership or corporation on the promissory notes of such individual, partnership or corporation secured by direct obligations of the United States. Such advances shall be made for periods not exceeding 90 days and shall bear interest at rates fixed from time to time by the Federal reserve bank, subject to the review and determination of the Federal Reserve Board."

Approved March 9th 1933 8.30 p. m.

4. "THOMAS" AMENDMENT, MAY 12, 1933

TITLE III—FINANCING—AND EXERCISING POWER CONFERRED BY SECTION 8 OF ARTICLE I OF THE CONSTITUTION: TO COIN MONEY AND TO REGULATE THE VALUE THEREOF

SEC. 43. Whenever the President finds, upon investigation, that (1) the foreign commerce of the United States is adversely affected by reason of the depreciation in the value of the currency of any other government or governments in relation to the present standard value of gold, or (2) action under this section is necessary in order to regulate and maintain the parity of currency issues of the United States, or (3) an economic emergency requires an expansion of credit, or (4) an expansion of credit is necessary to secure by international agreement a stabilization at proper levels of the currencies of various governments, the President is authorized, in his discretion—

(a) To direct the Secretary of the Treasury to enter into agreements with the several Federal Reserve banks and with the Federal Reserve Board whereby the Federal Reserve Board will, and it is hereby authorized to, notwithstanding any provisions of law or rules and regulations to the contrary, permit such reserve banks to agree that they will, (1) conduct, pursuant to existing law, throughout specified periods, open market operations in obligations of the United States Government or corporations in which the United States is the majority stockholder, and (2) purchase directly and hold in portfolio for an agreed period or periods of time Treasury bills or other obligations of the United States Government in an aggregate sum of $3,000,000,000 in addition to those they may then hold, unless prior to the termination of such period or periods the Secretary shall consent to their sale. No suspension of reserve requirements of the Federal Reserve banks, under the terms of section 11 (c) of the Federal Reserve Act, necessitated by reason of operations under this section, shall require the imposition of the graduated tax upon any deficiency in reserves as provided in said section 11 (c). Nor shall it require any automatic increase in the rates of interest or discount charged by any Federal Reserve bank, as otherwise specified in that section. The Federal Reserve Board, with the approval of the Secretary of the Treasury, may require the Federal Reserve banks to take such action as may be necessary, in the judgment of the Board and of the Secretary of the Treasury, to prevent undue credit expansion.

(b) If the Secretary, when directed by the President, is unable to secure the assent of the several Federal Reserve banks and the Federal Reserve Board to the agreements authorized in this section, or if operations under the above provisions prove to be inadequate to meet the purposes of this section, or if for any other reason additional measures are required in the judgment of the President to meet such purposes, then the President is authorized—

(1) To direct the Secretary of the Treasury to cause to be issued in such amount or amounts as he may from time to time order, United States notes, as provided in the Act entitled "An Act to authorize the issue of United States notes and for the redemption of funding thereof and for funding the floating debt of the United States", approved February 25, 1862, and Acts supplementary thereto and amendatory thereof, in the same size and of similar color to the Federal Reserve notes heretofore issued and in denominations of $1, $5, $10, $20, $50, $100, $500, $1,000, and $10,000; but notes issued under this subsection shall be issued only for the purpose of meeting maturing Federal obligations to repay sums borrowed by the United States and for purchasing United States bonds and other interest-bearing obligations of the United States: *Provided,* That when any such notes are used for such purpose the bond or other obligation so acquired or taken up shall be retired and canceled. Such notes shall be issued at such times and in such amounts as the President may approve but the aggregate amount of such notes outstanding at any time shall not exceed $3,000,000,000. There is hereby appropriated, out of any money in the Treasury not otherwise appropriated, an amount sufficient to enable the Secretary of the Treasury to retire and cancel 4 per centum annually of such outstanding notes, and the Secretary of the Treasury is hereby directed to retire and cancel annually 4 per centum of such outstanding notes. Such notes and all other coins and currencies heretofore or hereafter coined or issued by or under the authority of the United States shall be legal tender for all debts public and private.

(2) By proclamation to fix the weight of the gold dollar in grains nine tenths fine and also to fix the weight of the silver dollar in grains nine tenths fine at a definite fixed ratio in relation to the gold dollar at such amounts as he finds necessary from his investigation to stabilize domestic prices or to protect the foreign commerce against the adverse effect of depreciated foreign currencies, and to provide for the unlimited coinage of such gold and silver at the ratio so fixed, or in case the Government of the United States enters into an agreement with any government or governments under the terms of which the ratio between the value of gold and

other currency issued by the United States and by any such government or governments is established, the President may fix the weight of the gold dollar in accordance with the ratio so agreed upon, and such gold dollar, the weight of which is so fixed, shall be the standard unit of value, and all forms of money issued or coined by the United States shall be maintained at a parity with this standard and it shall be the duty of the Secretary of the Treasury to maintain such parity, but in no event shall the weight of the gold dollar be fixed so as to reduce its present weight by more than 50 per centum.

SEC. 44. The Secretary of the Treasury, with the approval of the President, is hereby authorized to make and promulgate rules and regulations covering any action taken or to be taken by the President under subsection (a) or (b) of section 43.

SEC. 45. (a) The President is authorized, for a period of six months from the date of the passage of this Act, to accept silver in payment of the whole or any part of the principal or interest now due, or to become due within six months after such date, from any foreign government or governments on account of any indebtedness to the United States, such silver to be accepted at not to exceed the price of 50 cents an ounce in United States currency. The aggregate value of the silver accepted under this section shall not exceed $200,000,000.

(b) The silver bullion accepted and received under the provisions of this section shall be subject to the requirements of existing law and the regulations of the mint service governing the methods of determining the amount of pure silver contained, and the amount of the charges or deductions, if any, to be made; but such silver bullion shall not be counted as part of the silver bullion authorized or required to be purchased and coined under the provisions of existing law.

(c) The silver accepted and received under the provisions of this section shall be deposited in the Treasury of the United States, to be held, used, and disposed of as in this section provided.

(d) The Secretary of the Treasury shall cause silver certificates to be issued in such denominations as he deems advisable to the total number of dollars for which such silver was accepted in payment of debts. Such silver certificates shall be used by the Treasurer of the United States in payment of any obligations of the United States.

(e) The silver so accepted and received under this section shall be coined into standard silver dollars and subsidiary coins sufficient, in the opinion of the Secretary of the Treasury, to meet any demands for redemption of such silver certificates issued under the provisions of this section, and such coins shall be retained in the

Treasury for the payment of such certificates on demand. The silver so accepted and received under this section, except so much thereof as is coined under the provisions of this section, shall be held in the Treasury for the sole purpose of aiding in maintaining the parity of such certificates as provided in existing law. Any such certificates or reissued certificates, when presented at the Treasury, shall be redeemed in standard silver dollars, or in subsidiary silver coin, at the option of the holder of the certificates: *Provided,* That, in the redemption of such silver certificates issued under this section, not to exceed one third of the coin required for such redemption may in the judgment of the Secretary of the Treasury be made in subsidiary coins, the balance to be made in standard silver dollars.

(f) When any silver certificates issued under the provisions of this section are redeemed or received into the Treasury from any source whatsoever, and belong to the United States, they shall not be retired, canceled, or destroyed, but shall be reissued and paid out again and kept in circulation; but nothing herein shall prevent the cancelation and destruction of mutilated certificates and the issue of other certificates of like denomination in their stead, as provided by law.

(g) The Secretary of the Treasury is authorized to make rules and regulations for carrying out the provisions of this section.

SEC. 46. Section 19 of the Federal Reserve Act, as amended, is amended by inserting immediately after paragraph (c) thereof the following new paragraph:

"Notwithstanding the foregoing provisions of this section, the Federal Reserve Board, upon the affirmative vote of not less than five of its members and with the approval of the President, may declare that an emergency exists by reason of credit expansion, and may by regulation during such emergency increase or decrease from time to time, in its discretion, the reserve balances required to be maintained against either demand or time deposits."

Approved May 12th 1933

5. ABROGATION OF THE GOLD CLAUSE, JUNE 5, 1933

JOINT RESOLUTION

To assure uniform value to the coins and currencies of the United States.

Whereas the holding of or dealing in gold affect the public interest, and are therefore subject to proper regulation and restriction; and Whereas the existing emergency has disclosed that provisions of obligations which purport to give the obligee a right to require payment in gold or a particular kind of coin or currency of the United States, or in an amount in money of the United States measured thereby, obstruct the power of the Congress to regulate the value of the money of the United States, and are inconsistent with the declared policy of the Congress to maintain at all times the equal power of every dollar, coined or issued by the United States, in the markets and in the payment of debts. Now, therefore, be it

Resolved by the Senate and House of Representatives of the United States of America in Congress assembled, That (a) every provision contained in or made with respect to any obligation which purports to give the obligee a right to require payment in gold or a particular kind of coin or currency, or in an amount in money of the United States measured thereby, is declared to be against public policy; and no such provision shall be contained in or made with respect to any obligation hereafter incurred. Every obligation, heretofore or hereafter incurred, whether or not any such provision is contained therein or made with respect thereto, shall be discharged upon payment, dollar for dollar, in any coin or currency which at the time of payment is legal tender for public and private debts. Any such provision contained in any law authorizing obligations to be issued by or under authority of the United States, is hereby repealed, but the repeal of any such provision shall not invalidate any other provision or authority contained in such law.

(b) As used in this resolution, the term "obligation" means an obligation (including every obligation of and to the United States, excepting currency) payable in money of the United States; and the term "coin or currency" means coin or currency of the United States, including Federal Reserve notes and circulating notes of Federal Reserve banks and national banking associations.

Sec. 2. The last sentence of paragraph (1) of subsection (b) of section 43 of the Act entitled "An Act to relieve the existing

146

national economic emergency by increasing agricultural purchasing power, to raise revenue for extraordinary expenses incurred by reason of such emergency, to provide emergency relief with respect to agricultural indebtedness, to provide for the orderly liquidation of joint-stock land banks, and for other purposes", approved May 12, 1933, is amended to read as follows:

"All coins and currencies of the United States (including Federal Reserve notes and circulating notes of Federal Reserve banks and national banking associations) heretofore or hereafter coined or issued, shall be legal tender for all debts, public and private, public charges, taxes, duties, and dues, except that gold coins, when below the standard weight and limit of tolerance provided by law for the single piece, shall be legal tender only at valuation in proportion to their actual weight."

Approved, June 5, 1933, 4.40 p.m.

6. GOLD RESERVE ACT, JANUARY 30, 1934

AN ACT

To protect the currency system of the United States, to provide for the better use of the monetary gold stock of the United States, and for other purposes.

Be it enacted by the Senate and House of Representatives of the United States of America in Congress assembled, That the short title of this Act shall be the "Gold Reserve Act of 1934."

SEC. 2. (a) Upon the approval of this Act all right, title, and interest, and every claim of the Federal Reserve Board, of every Federal Reserve bank, and of every Federal Reserve agent, in and to any and all gold coin and gold bullion shall pass to and are hereby vested in the United States; and in payment therefor credits in equivalent amounts in dollars are hereby established in the Treasury in the accounts authorized under the sixteenth paragraph of section 16 of the Federal Reserve Act, as heretofore and by this Act amended (U.S.C., title 12, sec. 467). Balances in such accounts shall be payable in gold certificates, which shall be in such form and in such denominations as the Secretary of the Treasury may determine. All gold so transferred, not in the possession of the United States, shall be held in custody for the United States and delivered upon the order of the Secretary of the Treasury; and the Federal Reserve Board, the Federal Reserve banks, and the Federal Reserve agents shall give such instructions and shall take such action as may be necessary to assure that such gold shall be so held and delivered.

(b) Section 16 of the Federal Reserve Act, as amended, is further amended in the following respects:

(1) The third sentence of the first paragraph is amended to read as follows: "They shall be redeemed in lawful money on demand at the Treasury Department of the United States, in the city of Washington, District of Columbia, or at any Federal Reserve bank."

(2) So much of the third sentence of the second paragraph as precedes the proviso is amended to read as follows: "The collateral security thus offered shall be notes, drafts, bills of exchange, or acceptances acquired under the provisions of section 13 of this Act, or bills of exchange endorsed by a member bank of any Federal Reserve district and purchased under the provisions of section 14 of this Act, or bankers' acceptances purchased under the provisions of said section 14, or gold certificates:"

(3) The first sentence of the third paragraph is amended to read as follows: "Every Federal Reserve bank shall maintain reserves in

gold certificates or lawful money of not less than 35 per centum against its deposits and reserves in gold certificates of not less than 40 per centum against its Federal Reserve notes in actual circulation: *Provided, however,* That when the Federal Reserve agent holds gold certificates as collateral for Federal Reserve notes issued to the bank such gold certificates shall be counted as part of the reserve which such bank is required to maintain against its Federal Reserve notes in actual circulation."

(4) The fifth and sixth sentences of the third paragraph are amended to read as follows: "Notes presented for redemption at the Treasury of the United States shall be paid out of the redemption fund and returned to the Federal Reserve banks through which they were originally issued, and thereupon such Federal Reserve bank shall, upon demand of the Secretary of the Treasury, reimburse such redemption fund in lawful money or, if such Federal Reserve notes have been redeemed by the Treasurer in gold certificates, then such funds shall be reimbursed to the extent deemed necessary by the Secretary of the Treasury in gold certificates, and such Federal Reserve bank shall, so long as any of its Federal Reserve notes remain outstanding, maintain with the Treasurer in gold certificates an amount sufficient in the judgment of the Secretary to provide for all redemptions to be made by the Treasurer. Federal Reserve notes received by the Treasurer otherwise than for redemption may be exchanged for gold certificates out of the redemption fund hereinafter provided and returned to the Reserve bank through which they were originally issued, or they may be returned to such bank for the credit of the United States."

(5) The fourth, fifth, and sixth paragraphs are amended to read as follows:

"The Federal Reserve Board shall require each Federal Reserve bank to maintain on deposit in the Treasury of the United States a sum in gold certificates sufficient in the judgment of the Secretary of the Treasury for the redemption of the Federal Reserve notes issued to such bank, but in no event less than 5 per centum of the total amount of notes issued less the amount of gold certificates held by the Federal Reserve agent as collateral security; but such deposit of gold certificates shall be counted and included as part of the 40 per centum reserve hereinbefore required. The Board shall have the right, acting through the Federal Reserve agent, to grant in whole or in part, or to reject entirely the application of any Federal Reserve bank for Federal Reserve notes; but to the extent that such application may be granted the Federal Reserve Board shall, through its local Federal Reserve agent, supply Federal Reserve notes to the banks so applying, and such bank shall be charged with the amount of the notes issued to it and shall pay such rate of interest as may be established by the Federal Reserve Board on only that amount of such notes which equals the total amount of its outstanding Federal Reserve notes less the amount of gold certificates held by the Federal Reserve agent as collateral security. Federal Reserve notes issued to any such bank shall, upon delivery, together with such notes of such Federal Reserve bank as may be issued under section 18 of this Act upon security of United States 2 per centum Government bonds, become a first and paramount lien on all the assets of such bank.

"Any Federal Reserve bank may at any time reduce its liability for outstanding Federal Reserve notes by depositing with the Federal Reserve agent its Federal Reserve notes, gold certificates, or lawful money of the United States. Federal Reserve notes so deposited shall not be reissued, except upon compliance with the conditions of an original issue.

"The Federal Reserve agent shall hold such gold certificates or lawful money available exclusively for exchange for the outstanding Federal Reserve notes when offered by the Reserve bank of which he is a director. Upon the request of the Secretary of the Treasury the Federal Reserve Board shall require the Federal Reserve agent to transmit to the Treasurer of the United States so much of the gold certificates held by him as collateral security for Federal Reserve notes as may be required for the exclusive purpose of the redemption of such Federal Reserve notes, but such gold certificates when deposited with the Treasurer shall be counted and considered as if collateral security on deposit with the Federal Reserve agent."

(6) The eighth paragraph is amended to read as follows:

"All Federal Reserve notes and all gold certificates and lawful money issued to or deposited with any Federal Reserve agent under the provisions of the Federal Reserve Act shall hereafter be held for such agent, under such rules and regulations as the Federal Reserve Board may prescribe, in the joint custody of himself and the Federal Reserve bank to which he is accredited. Such agent and such Federal Reserve bank shall be jointly liable for the safekeeping of such Federal Reserve notes, gold certificates, and lawful money. Nothing herein contained, however, shall be construed to prohibit a Federal Reserve agent from depositing gold certificates with the Federal Reserve Board, to be held by such Board subject to his order, or with the Treasurer of the United States for the purposes authorized by law."

(7) The sixteenth paragraph is amended to read as follows:

"The Secretary of the Treasury is hereby authorized and directed to receive deposits of gold or of gold certificates with the Treasurer or any Assistant Treasurer of the United States when tendered by any Federal Reserve bank or Federal Reserve agent for credit to its or his account with the Federal Reserve Board. The Secretary shall prescribe by regulation the form of receipt to be issued by the Treasurer or Assistant Treasurer to the Federal Reserve bank or Federal Reserve agent making the deposit, and a duplicate of such receipt shall be delivered to the Federal Reserve Board by the Treasurer at Washington upon proper advices from any Assistant Treasurer that such deposit has been made. Deposits so made shall be held subject to the orders of the Federal Reserve Board and shall be payable in gold certificates on the order of the Federal Reserve Board to any Federal Reserve bank or Federal Reserve agent at the Treasury or at the Subtreasury of the United States nearest the place of business of such Federal Reserve bank or such Federal Reserve agent. The order used by the Federal Reserve Board in making such payments shall be signed by the governor or vice governor, or such other officers or members as the Board may by regulation prescribe. The form of such order shall be approved by the Secretary of the Treasury."

(8) The eighteenth paragraph is amended to read as follows:

"Deposits made under this section standing to the credit of any Federal Reserve bank with the Federal Reserve Board shall, at the option of said bank, be counted as part of the lawful reserve which it is required to maintain against outstanding Federal Reserve notes, or as a part of the reserve it is required to maintain against deposits."

SEC. 3. The Secretary of the Treasury shall, by regulations issued hereunder, with the approval of the President, prescribe the conditions under which gold may be acquired and held, transported, melted or treated, imported, exported, or earmarked: (a) for industrial, professional, and artistic use; (b) by the Federal Reserve banks for the purpose of settling international balances; and, (c) for such other purposes as in his judgment are not inconsistent with the purposes of this Act. Gold in any form may be acquired, transported, melted or treated, imported, exported, or earmarked or held in custody for foreign or domestic account (except on behalf of the United States) only to the extent permitted by, and subject to the conditions prescribed in, or pursuant to, such regulations. Such regulations may exempt from the provisions of this section, in whole or in part, gold situated in the Philippine Islands or other places beyond the limits of the continental United States.

SEC. 4. Any gold withheld, acquired, transported, melted or treated, imported, exported, or earmarked or held in custody, in violation of this Act or of any regulations issued hereunder, or licenses issued pursuant thereto, shall be forfeited to the United

States, and may be seized and condemned by like proceedings as those provided by law for the forfeiture, seizure, and condemnation of property imported into the United States contrary to law; and in addition any person failing to comply with the provisions of this Act or of any such regulations or licenses, shall be subject to a penalty equal to twice the value of the gold in respect of which such failure occurred.

SEC. 5. No gold shall hereafter be coined, and no gold coin shall hereafter be paid out or delivered by the United States: *Provided, however,* That coinage may continue to be executed by the mints of the United States for foreign countries in accordance with the Act of January 29, 1874 (U.S.C., title 31, sec. 367). All gold coin of the United States shall be withdrawn from circulation, and, together with all other gold owned by the United States, shall be formed into bars of such weights and degrees of fineness as the Secretary of the Treasury may direct.

SEC. 6. Except to the extent permitted in regulations which may be issued hereunder by the Secretary of the Treasury with the approval of the President, no currency of the United States shall be redeemed in gold: *Provided, however,* That gold certificates owned by the Federal Reserve banks shall be redeemed at such times and in such amounts as, in the judgment of the Secretary of the Treasury, are necessary to maintain the equal purchasing power of every kind of currency of the United States: *And provided further,* That the reserve for United States notes and for Treasury notes of 1890, and the security for gold certificates (including the gold certificates held in the Treasury for credits payable therein) shall be maintained in gold bullion equal to the dollar amounts required by law, and the reserve for Federal Reserve notes shall be maintained in gold certificates, or in credits payable in gold certificates maintained with the Treasurer of the United States under section 16 of the Federal Reserve Act, as heretofore and by this Act amended.

No redemptions in gold shall be made except in gold bullion bearing the stamp of a United States mint or assay office in an amount equivalent at the time of redemption to the currency surrendered for such purpose.

SEC. 7. In the event that the weight of the gold dollar shall at any time be reduced, the resulting increase in value of the gold held by the United States (including the gold held as security for gold certificates and as a reserve for any United States notes and for Treasury notes of 1890) shall be covered into the Treasury as a miscellaneous receipt; and, in the event that the weight of the gold dollar shall at any time be increased, the resulting decrease in value of the gold held as a reserve for any United States notes and for Treasury notes of 1890, and as security for gold certificates shall be compensated by transfers of gold bullion from the general fund, and there is hereby appropriated an amount sufficient to provide for such transfers and to cover the decrease in value of the gold in the general fund.

SEC. 8. Section 3700 of the Revised Statutes (U.S.C., title 31, sec. 734) is amended to read as follows:

"SEC. 3700. With the approval of the President, the Secretary of the Treasury may purchase gold in any amounts, at home or abroad, with any direct obligations, coin, or currency of the United States, authorized by law, or with any funds in the Treasury not otherwise appropriated, at such rates and upon such terms and conditions as he may deem most advantageous to the public interest; any provision of law relating to the maintenance of parity, or limiting the purposes for which any of such obligations, coin, or currency, may be issued, or requiring any such obligations to be offered as a popular loan or on a competitive basis, or to be offered or issued at not less than par, to the contrary notwithstanding. All gold so purchased shall be included as an asset of the general fund of the Treasury."

SEC. 9. Section 3699 of the Revised Statutes (U.S.C., title 31, sec. 733) is amended to read as follows:

"SEC. 3699. The Secretary of the Treasury may anticipate the payment of interest on the public debt, by a period not exceeding one year, from time to time, either with or without a rebate of interest upon the coupons, as to him may seem expedient; and he may sell gold in any amounts, at home or abroad, in such manner and at such rates and upon such terms and conditions as he may deem most advantageous to the public interest, and the proceeds of any gold so sold shall be covered into the general fund of the Treasury: *Provided, however,* That the Secretary of the Treasury may sell the gold which is required to be maintained as a reserve or as security for currency issued by the United States, only to the extent necessary to maintain such currency at a parity with the gold dollar."

SEC. 10. (a) For the purpose of stabilizing the exchange value of the dollar, the Secretary of the Treasury, with the approval of the President, directly or through such agencies as he may designate, is authorized, for the account of the fund established in this section, to deal in gold and foreign exchange and such other instruments of credit and securities as he may deem necessary to carry out the purpose of this section. An annual audit of such fund shall be made and a report thereof submitted to the President.

(b) To enable the Secretary of the Treasury to carry out the provisions of this section there is hereby appropriated, out of the receipts which are directed to be covered into the Treasury under section 7 hereof, the sum of $2,000,000,000, which sum when available shall be deposited with the Treasurer of the United States in a stabilization fund (hereinafter called the "fund") under the exclusive control of the Secretary of the Treasury, with the approval of the President, whose decisions shall be final and not be subject to review by any other officer of the United States. The fund shall be available for expenditure, under the direction of the Secretary of the Treasury and in his discretion, for any purpose in connection with carrying out the provisions of this section, including the investment and reinvestment in direct obligations of the United States of any portions of the fund which the Secretary of the Treasury, with the approval of the President, may from time to time determine are not currently required for stabilizing the exchange value of the dollar. The proceeds of all sales and investments and all earnings and interest accruing under the operations of this section shall be paid into the fund and shall be available for the purposes of the fund.

(c) All the powers conferred by this section shall expire two years after the date of enactment of this Act, unless the President shall sooner declare the existing emergency ended and the operation of the stabilization fund terminated; but the President may extend such period for not more than one additional year after such date by proclamation recognizing the continuance of such emergency.

SEC. 11. The Secretary of the Treasury is hereby authorized to issue, with the approval of the President, such rules and regulations as the Secretary may deem necessary or proper to carry out the purposes of this Act.

SEC. 12. Paragraph (b) (2), of section 43, title III, of the Act approved May 12, 1933 (Public, Numbered 10, Seventy-third Congress), is amended by adding two new sentences at the end thereof, reading as follows:

"Nor shall the weight of the gold dollar be fixed in any event at more than 60 per centum of its present weight. The powers of the President specified in this paragraph shall be deemed to be separate, distinct, and continuing powers, and may be exercised by him, from time to time, severally or together, whenever and as the expressed objects of this section in his judgment may require; except that such powers shall expire two years after the date of enactment of the Gold Reserve Act of 1934 unless the President shall sooner declare the existing emergency ended, but the President may extend such period for not more than one additional year after such date by proclamation recognizing the continuance of such emergency."

Paragraph (2) of subsection (b) of section 43, title III, of an Act entitled "An Act to relieve the existing national economic emergency by increasing agricultural purchasing power, to raise revenue for extraordinary expenses incurred by reason of such emergency, to provide emergency relief with respect to agricultural indebtedness, to provide for the orderly liquidation of joint-stock land banks, and for other purposes", approved May 12, 1933, is amended by adding at the end of said paragraph (2) the following:

"The President, in addition to the authority to provide for the unlimited coinage of silver at the ratio so fixed, under such terms and conditions as he may prescribe, is further authorized to cause to be issued and delivered to the tenderer of silver for coinage, silver certificates in lieu of the standard silver dollars to which the tenderer would be entitled and in an amount in dollars equal to the number of coined standard silver dollars that the tenderer of such silver for coinage would receive in standard silver dollars.

"The President is further authorized to issue silver certificates in such denominations as he may prescribe against any silver bullion, silver, or standard silver dollars in the Treasury not then held for redemption of any outstanding silver certificates, and to coin standard silver dollars or subsidiary currency for the redemption of such silver certificates.

"The President is authorized, in his discretion, to prescribe different terms and conditions and to make different charges, or to collect different seigniorage, for the coinage of silver of foreign production than for the coinage of silver produced in the United States or its dependencies. The silver certificates herein referred to shall be issued, delivered, and circulated substantially in conformity with the law now governing existing silver certificates, except as may herein be expressly provided to the contrary, and shall have and possess all of the privileges and the legal tender characteristics of existing silver certificates now in the Treasury of the United States, or in circulation.

"The President is authorized, in addition to other powers, to reduce the weight of the standard silver dollar in the same percentage that he reduces the weight of the gold dollar.

"The President is further authorized to reduce and fix the weight of subsidiary coins so as to maintain the parity of such coins with the standard silver dollar and with the gold dollar."

SEC. 13. All actions, regulations, rules, orders, and proclamations heretofore taken, promulgated, made or issued by the President of the United States or the Secretary of the Treasury, under the Act of March 9, 1933, or under section 43 or section 45 of title III of the Act of May 12, 1933, are hereby approved, ratified, and confirmed.

SEC. 14. (a) The Second Liberty Bond Act, as amended, is further amended as follows:

(1) By adding at the end of section 1 (U.S.C., title 31, sec. 752; Supp. VII, title 31, sec. 752), a new paragraph as follows:

"Notwithstanding the provisions of the foregoing paragraph, the Secretary of the Treasury may from time to time, when he deems it to be in the public interest, offer such bonds otherwise than as a popular loan and he may make allotments in full, or reject or reduce allotments upon any applications whether or not the offering was made as a popular loan."

(2) By inserting in section 8 (U.S.C., title 31, sec. 771), after the words "certificates of indebtedness", a comma and the words "Treasury bills".

(3) By striking out the figures "$7,500,000,000" where they appear in section 18 (U.S.C., title 31, sec. 753) and inserting in lieu thereof the figures "$10,000,000,000."

(4) By adding thereto two new sections, as follows:

"SEC. 19. Notwithstanding any other provisions of law, any obligations authorized by this Act may be issued for the purchase, redemption, or refunding, at or before maturity, of any outstanding bonds, notes, certificates of indebtedness, or Treasury bills, of the United States, or to obtain funds for such purchase, redemption, or refunding, under such rules, regulations, terms, and conditions as the Secretary of the Treasury may prescribe.

"SEC. 20. The Secretary of the Treasury may issue any obligations authorized by this Act and maturing not more than one year from the date of their issue on a discount basis and payable at maturity without interest. Any such obligations may also be offered for sale on a competitive basis under such regulations and upon such terms and conditions as the Secretary of the Treasury may prescribe, and the decisions of the Secretary in respect of any issue shall be final."

(b) Section 6 of the Victory Liberty Loan Act (U.S.C., title 31, sec. 767; Supp. VII, title 31, secs. 767–767a) is amended by striking out the words "for refunding purposes", together with the preceding comma, at the end of the first sentence of subsection (a).

(c) The Secretary of the Treasury is authorized to issue gold certificates in such form and in such denominations as he may determine, against any gold held by the Treasurer of the United States, except the gold fund held as a reserve for any United States notes and Treasury notes of 1890. The amount of gold certificates issued and outstanding shall at no time exceed the value, at the legal standard, of the gold so held against gold certificates.

SEC. 15. As used in this Act the term "United States" means the Government of the United States; the term "the continental United States" means the States of the United States, the District of Columbia, and the Territory of Alaska; the term "currency of the United States" means currency which is legal tender in the United States, and includes United States notes, Treasury notes of 1890, gold certificates, silver certificates, Federal Reserve notes, and circulating notes of Federal Reserve banks and national banking associations; and the term "person" means any individual, partnership, association, or corporation, including the Federal Reserve Board, Federal Reserve banks, and Federal Reserve agents. Wherever reference is made in this Act to equivalents as between dollars or currency of the United States and gold, one dollar or one dollar face amount of any currency of the United States equals such a number of grains of gold, nine tenths fine, as, at the time referred to, are contained in the standard unit of value, that is, so long as the President shall not have altered by proclamation the weight of the gold dollar under the authority of section 43, title III, of the Act approved May 12, 1933, as heretofore and by this Act amended, twenty-five and eight tenths grains of gold, nine tenths fine, and thereafter such a number of grains of gold, nine tenths fine, as the President shall have fixed under such authority.

SEC. 16. The right to alter, amend, or repeal this Act is hereby expressly reserved. If any provision of this Act, or the application thereof to any person or circumstances, is held invalid, the remainder of the Act, and the application of such provision to other persons or circumstances, shall not be affected thereby.

SEC. 17. All Acts and parts of Acts inconsistent with any of the provisions of this Act are hereby repealed.

Approved, January 30, 1934.

7. SILVER PURCHASE ACT, JUNE 19, 1934

AN ACT

To authorize the Secretary of the Treasury to purchase silver, issue silver certificates, and for other purposes.

Be it enacted by the Senate and House of Representatives of the United States of America in Congress assembled, That the short title of this Act shall be the "Silver Purchase Act of 1934."

SEC. 2. It is hereby declared to be the policy of the United States that the proportion of silver to gold in the monetary stocks of the United States should be increased, with the ultimate objective of having and maintaining, one fourth of the monetary value of such stocks in silver.

SEC. 3. Whenever and so long as the proportion of silver in the stocks of gold and silver of the United States is less than one-fourth of the monetary value of such stocks, the Secretary of the Treasury is authorized and directed to purchase silver, at home or abroad, for present or future delivery with any direct obligations, coin, or currency of the United States, authorized by law, or with any funds in the Treasury not otherwise appropriated, at such rates, at such times, and upon such terms and conditions as he may deem reasonable and most advantageous to the public interest: *Provided,* That no purchase of silver shall be made hereunder at a price in excess of the monetary value thereof: *And provided further,* That no purchases of silver situated in the continental United States on May 1, 1934, shall be made hereunder at a price in excess of 50 cents a fine ounce.

SEC. 4. Whenever and so long as the market price of silver exceeds its monetary value or the monetary value of the stocks of silver is greater than 25 per centum of the monetary value of the stocks of gold and silver, the Secretary of the Treasury may, with the approval of the President and subject to the provisions of section 5, sell any silver acquired under the authority of this Act, at home or abroad, for present or future delivery, at such rates, at such times, and upon such terms and conditions as he may deem reasonable and most advantageous to the public interest.

SEC. 5. The Secretary of the Treasury is authorized and directed to issue silver certificates in such denominations as he may from time to time prescribe in a face amount not less than the cost of all silver purchased under the authority of section 3, and such certificates shall be placed in actual circulation. There shall be maintained in the Treasury as security for all silver certificates heretofore or hereafter issued and at the time outstanding an amount of silver in bullion and standard silver dollars of a monetary value equal to the face amount of such silver certificates. All silver certificates heretofore or hereafter issued shall be legal tender for all debts, public and private, public charges, taxes, duties, and dues, and shall be redeemable on demand at the Treasury of the United States in standard silver dollars; and the Secretary of the Treasury is authorized to coin standard silver dollars for such redemption.

SEC. 6. Whenever in his judgment such action is necessary to effectuate the policy of this Act, the Secretary of the Treasury is authorized, with the approval of the President, to investigate, regulate, or prohibit, by means of licenses or otherwise, the acquisition, importation, exportation, or transportation of silver and of contracts and other arrangements made with respect thereto; and to require the filing of reports deemed by him reasonably necessary in connection therewith. Whoever willfully violates the provisions of any license, order, rule, or regulation issued pursuant to the authorization contained in this section shall, upon conviction, be fined not more than $10,000 or, if a natural person, may be imprisoned for not more than ten years, or both; and any officer, director, or agent of any corporation who knowingly participates in such violation may be punished by a like fine, imprisonment, or both.

SEC. 7. Whenever in the judgment of the President such action is necessary to effectuate the policy of this Act, he may by Executive order require the delivery to the United States mints of any or all silver by whomever owned or possessed. The silver so delivered shall be coined into standard silver dollars or otherwise added to the monetary stocks of the United States as the President may determine; and there shall be returned therefor in standard silver dollars, or any other coin or currency of the United States, the monetary value of the silver so delivered less such deductions for seigniorage, brassage, coinage, and other mint charges as the Secretary of the Treasury with the approval of the President shall have determined: *Provided,* That in no case shall the value of the amount returned therefor be less than the fair value at the time of such order of the silver required to be delivered as such value is determined by the market price over a reasonable period terminating at the time of such order. The Secretary of the Treasury shall pay all necessary costs of the transportation of such silver and standard silver dollars, coin, or currency, including the cost of insurance, protection, and such other incidental costs as may be reasonably necessary. Any silver withheld in violation of any Executive order issued under this section or of any regulations issued pursuant thereto shall be forfeited to the United States, and may be seized and condemned by like proceedings as those provided by law for the forfeiture, seizure, and condemnation of property imported into the United States contrary to law; and, in addition, any person failing to comply with the provisions of any such Executive order or regulation shall be subject to a penalty equal to twice the monetary value of the silver in respect of which such failure occurred.

SEC. 8. Schedule A of title VIII of the Revenue Act of 1926, as amended (relating to stamp taxes), is amended by adding at the end thereof a new subdivision to read as follows:

"10. SILVER, AND SO FORTH, SALES AND TRANSFERS.—On all transfers of any interest in silver bullion, if the price for which such interest is or is to be transferred exceeds the total of the cost thereof and allowed expenses, 50 per centum of the amount of such excess. On every such transfer there shall be made and delivered by the transferor to the transferee a memorandum to which there shall be affixed lawful stamps in value equal to the tax thereon. Every such memorandum shall show the date thereof, the names and addresses of the transferor and transferee, the interest in silver bullion to which it refers, the price for which such interest is or is to be transferred and the cost thereof and the allowed expenses. Any person liable for payment of tax under this subdivision (or anyone who acts in the matter as agent or broker for any such person) who is a party to any such transfer, or who in pursuance of any such transfer delivers any silver bullion or interest therein, without a memorandum stating truly and completely the information herein required, or who delivers any such memorandum without having the proper stamps affixed thereto, with intent to evade the foregoing provisions, shall be deemed guilty of a misdemeanor, and upon conviction thereof shall pay a fine of not exceeding $1,000 or be imprisoned not more than six months, or both. Stamps affixed under this subdivision shall be canceled (in lieu of the manner provided in section 804) by such officers and in such manner as regulations under this subdivision shall prescribe. Such officers shall cancel such stamps only if it appears that the proper tax is being paid, and when stamps with respect to any transfer are so canceled, the transferor and not the transferee shall be liable for any additional tax found due or penalty with respect to such transfer. The Commissioner shall abate or refund, in accordance with regulations issued hereunder, such portion of any tax hereunder as he finds to be attributable to profits (1) realized in the course of the transferor's regular business of furnishing silver bullion for industrial, professional, or artistic use and (a) not resulting from a change in the market price of silver bullion, or (b) offset by contemporaneous losses incurred in transactions in interests in silver bullion determined, in accordance with such regulations, to have been specifically related hedging transactions; or (2) offset by contemporaneous losses attributable to changes in the market price of silver bullion and incurred in transactions in silver foreign exchange determined, in accordance with such regulations, to have been hedged specifically by the interest in silver bullion transferred. The provisions of this subdivision shall extend to all transfers in the United States of any interest in silver bullion, and to all such transfers outside the United States if either party thereto is a resident of the United States or is a citizen of the United States who has been a resident thereof within three months before the date of the transfer or if such silver bullion or interest therein is situated in the United States; and shall extend to transfers to the United States Government (the tax in such cases to be payable by the transferor), but shall not extend to transfers of silver bullion by deposit or delivery at a United States mint under proclamation by the President or in compliance with any Executive order issued pursuant to section 7 of the Silver Purchase Act of 1934. The tax under this subdivision on transfers enumerated in subdivision 4 shall be in addition to the tax under such subdivision. This subdivision shall apply (1) with respect to all transfers of any interest in silver bullion after the enactment of the Silver Purchase Act of 1934, and (2) with respect to all transfers of any interest in silver bullion on or after May 15, 1934, and prior to the enactment of the Silver Purchase Act of 1934, except that in such cases it shall be paid by the transferor in such manner and at such time as the Commissioner, with the approval of the Secretary of the Treasury, may by regulations prescribe, and the requirement of a memorandum of such transfer shall not apply.

"As used in this subdivision—

"The term 'cost' means the cost of the interest in silver bullion to the transferor, except that (a) in case of silver bullion produced from materials containing silver which has not previously entered into industrial, commercial, or monetary use, the cost to a transferor who is the producer shall be deemed to be the market price at the time of production determined in accordance with regulations issued hereunder; (b) in the case of an interest in silver bullion acquired by the transferor otherwise than for valuable consideration, the cost shall be deemed to be the cost thereof to the last previous transferor by whom it was acquired for a valuable consideration; and (c) in the case of any interest in silver bullion acquired by the transferor (after April 15, 1934) in a wash sale, the cost shall be deemed to be the cost to him of the interest transferred by him in such wash sale, but with proper adjustment, in accordance with regulations under this subdivision, when such interests are in silver bullion for delivery at different times.

"The term 'transfer' means a sale, agreement of sale, agreement to sell, memorandum of sale or delivery of, or transfer, whether made by assignment in blank or by any delivery, or by any paper or agreement or memorandum or any other evidence of transfer or sale; or means to make a transfer as so defined.

"The term 'interest in silver bullion' means any title or claim to, or interest in, any silver bullion or contract therefor.

"The term 'allowed expenses' means usual and necessary expenses actually incurred in holding, processing, or transporting the interest in silver bullion as to which an interest is transferred (including storage, insurance, and transportation charges but not including interest, taxes, or charges in the nature of overhead), determined in accordance with regulations issued hereunder.

"The term 'memorandum' means a bill, memorandum, agreement, or other evidence of a transfer.

"The term 'wash sale' means a transaction involving the transfer of an interest in silver bullion and, within thirty days before or after such transfer, the acquisition by the same person of an interest in silver bullion. Only so much of the interest so acquired as does not exceed the interest so transferred, and only so much of the interest so transferred as does not exceed the interest so acquired, shall be deemed to be included in the wash sale.

"The term 'silver bullion' means silver which has been melted, smelted, or refined and is in such state or condition that its value depends primarily upon the silver content and not upon its form."

Sec. 9. The Secretary of the Treasury is hereby authorized to issue, with the approval of the President, such rules and regulations as the Secretary of the Treasury may deem necessary or proper to carry out the purposes of this Act, or of any order issued hereunder.

Sec. 10. As used in this Act—

The term "person" means an individual, partnership, association, or corporation;

The term "the continental United States" means the States of the United States, the District of Columbia, and the Territory of Alaska;

The term "monetary value" means a value calculated on the basis of $1 for an amount of silver or gold equal to the amount at the time contained in the standard silver dollar and the gold dollar, respectively;

The term "stocks of silver" means the total amount of silver at the time owned by the United States (whether or not held as security for outstanding currency of the United States) and of silver contained in coins of the United States at the time outstanding;

The term "stocks of gold" means the total amount of gold at the time owned by the United States, whether or not held as a reserve or as security for any outstanding currency of the United States.

SEC. 11. There is authorized to be appropriated, out of any money in the Treasury not otherwise appropriated, the sum of $500,000, which shall be available for expenditure under the direction of the President and in his discretion, for any purpose in connection with the carrying out of this Act; and there are hereby authorized to be appropriated annually such additional sums as may be necessary for such purposes.

SEC. 12. The right to alter, amend, or repeal this Act is hereby expressly reserved. If any provision of this Act, or the application thereof to any person or circumstances, is held invalid, the remainder of the Act, and the application of such provision to other persons or circumstances, shall not be affected thereby.

SEC. 13. All Acts and parts of Acts inconsistent with any of the provisions of this Act are hereby repealed, but the authority conferred in this Act upon the President and the Secretary of the Treasury is declared to be supplemental to the authority heretofore conferred.

Approved, June 19, 1934, 9 P.M.

8. BANK HOLIDAY PROCLAMATION, MARCH 6, 1933

BY THE PRESIDENT OF THE UNITED STATES OF AMERICA

A PROCLAMATION

WHEREAS there have been heavy and unwarranted withdrawals of gold and currency from our banking institutions for the purpose of hoarding; and

WHEREAS continuous and increasingly extensive speculative activity abroad in foreign exchange has resulted in severe drains on the Nation's stocks of gold; and

WHEREAS those conditions have created a national emergency; and

WHEREAS it is in the best interests of all bank depositors that a period of respite be provided with a view to preventing further hoarding of coin, bullion or currency or speculation in foreign exchange and permitting the application of appropriate measures to protect the interests of our people; and

WHEREAS it is provided in Section 5 (b) of the Act of October 6, 1917 (40 Stat.L.411) as amended, "That the President may investigate, regulate, or prohibit, under such rules and regulations as he may prescribe, by means of licenses or otherwise, any transactions in foreign exchange and the export, hoarding, melting, or earmarkings of gold or silver coin or bullion or currency ***"; and

WHEREAS it is provided in Section 16 of the said Act "that whoever shall willfully violate any of the provisions of this Act or of any license, rule, or regulation issued thereunder, and whoever shall willfully violate, neglect, or refuse to comply with any order of the President issued in compliance with the provisions of this Act, shall, upon conviction, be fined not more than $10,000, or, if a natural person, imprisoned for not more than ten years, or both; ***";

NOW, THEREFORE, I, FRANKLIN D. ROOSEVELT, President of the United States of America, in view of such national emergency and by virtue of the authority vested in me by said Act and in order to prevent the export, hoarding, or earmarking of gold or silver coin or bullion or currency, do hereby proclaim, order, direct and declare that from Monday, the sixth day of March, to Thursday, the ninth day of March, Nineteen Hundred and Thirty Three, both dates inclusive, there shall be maintained and observed by all banking institutions and all branches thereof located in the United States of America, including the territories and insular possessions, a bank holiday, and that during said period all banking transactions shall be suspended. During such holiday, excepting as hereinafter provided, no such banking institution or branch shall pay out, export, earmark, or permit the withdrawal or transfer in any manner or by any device whatsoever, of any gold or silver coin or bullion or currency or take any other action which might facilitate the hoarding thereof; nor shall any such banking institution or branch pay out deposits, make loans or discounts, deal in foreign exchange, transfer credits from the United States to any place abroad, or transact any other banking business whatsoever.

During such holiday, the Secretary of the Treasury, with the approval of the President and under such regulations as he may prescribe, is authorized and empowered (a) to permit any or all of such banking institutions to perform any or all of the usual banking functions, (b) to direct, require or permit the issuance of clearing house certificates or other evidences of claims against assets of banking institutions, and (c) to authorize and direct the creation in such banking institutions of special trust accounts for the receipt of new deposits which shall be subject to withdrawal on demand without any restriction or limitation and shall be kept separately in cash or on deposit in Federal Reserve Banks or invested in obligations of the United States.

As used in this order the term "banking institutions" shall include all Federal Reserve banks, national banking associations, banks, trust companies, savings banks, building and loan associations, credit unions, or other corporations, partnerships, associations or persons, engaged in the business of receiving deposits, making loans, discounting business paper, or transacting any other form of banking business.

IN WITNESS WHEREOF, I have hereunto set my hand and caused the seal of the United States to be affixed.

Done in the City of Washington this 6th day of March—1 A.M. in the year of our Lord One Thousand Nine Hundred and Thirty-three, and of the Independence of the United States the One Hundred and Fifty-seventh.

(SEAL)

FRANKLIN D. ROOSEVELT

By the President:

CORDELL HULL
Secretary of State

9. PRESIDENT'S MESSAGE TO LONDON ECONOMIC CONFERENCE, JULY 2, 1933

DEPARTMENT OF STATE

FOR THE PRESS   July 3, 1933

The Secretary of State, Mr. Cordell Hull, at London, in his capacity as Secretary of State, today made public the following message to him from the President of the United States, dated July 2, 1933:

"I would regard it as a catastrophe amounting to a world tragedy if the great Conference of Nations, called to bring about a more real and permanent financial stability and a greater prosperity to the masses of all nations, should, in advance of any serious effort to consider these broader problems, allow itself to be diverted by the proposal of a purely artificial and temporary experiment affecting the monetary exchange of a few nations only. Such action, such diversion, shows a singular lack of proportion and a failure to remember the larger purposes for which the Economic Conference originally was called together.

"I do not relish the thought that insistence on such action should be made an excuse for the continuance of the basic economic errors that underlie so much of the present world wide depression.

"The world will not long be lulled by the specious fallacy of achieving a temporary and probably an artificial stability in foreign exchange on the part of a few large countries only.

"The sound internal economic system of a nation is a greater factor in its well being than the price of its currency in changing terms of the currencies of other nations.

"It is for this reason that reduced cost of government, adequate government income, and ability to service government debts are all so important to ultimate stability. So too, old fetishes of so-called international bankers are being replaced by efforts to plan national currencies with the objective of giving to those currencies a continuing purchasing power which does not greatly vary in terms of the commodities and need of modern civilization. Let me be frank in saying that the United States seeks the kind of a dollar which a generation hence will have the same purchasing and debt paying power as the dollar value we hope to attain in the near future. That objective means more to the good of other nations than a fixed ratio for a month or two in terms of the pound or franc.

"Our broad purpose is the permanent stabilization of every nation's currency. Gold or gold and silver can well continue to be a metallic reserve behind currencies but this is not the time to dissipate gold reserves. When the world works out concerted policies in the majority of nations to produce balanced budgets and living within their means, then we can properly discuss a better distribution of the world's gold and silver supply to act as a reserve base of national currencies. Restoration of world trade is an important partner, both in the means and in the result. Here also temporary exchange fixing is not the true answer. We must rather mitigate existing embargoes to make easier the exchange of products which one nation has and the other nation has not.

"The Conference was called to better and perhaps to cure fundamental economic ills. It must not be diverted from that effort."

10. EXTRACT FROM PRESIDENT'S RADIO SPEECH, OCTOBER 22, 1933

Finally, I repeat what I have said on many occasions, that ever since last March the definite policy of the Government has been to restore commodity price levels. The object has been the attainment of such a level as will enable agriculture and industry once more to give work to the unemployed. It has been to make possible the payment of public and private debts more nearly at the price level at which they were incurred. It has been gradually to restore a balance in the price structure so that farmers may exchange their products for the products of industry on a fairer exchange basis. It has been and is also the purpose to prevent prices from rising beyond the point necessary to attain these ends. The permanent welfare and security of every class of our people ultimately depends on our attainment of these purposes.

Obviously, and because hundreds of different kinds of crops and industrial occupations in the huge territory that makes up this Nation are involved, we cannot reach the goal in only a few months. We may take one year or two years or three years.

No one who considers the plain facts of our situation believes that commodity prices, especially agricultural prices, are high enough yet.

Some people are putting the cart before the horse. They want a permanent revaluation of the dollar first. It is the Government's policy to restore the price level first. I would not know, and no one else could tell, just what the permanent valuation of the dollar will be. To guess at a permanent gold valuation now would certainly require later changes caused by later facts.

When we have restored the price level, we shall seek to establish and maintain a dollar which will not change its purchasing and debt paying power during the succeeding generation. I said that in my message to the American delegation in London last July. And I say it now once more.

Because of conditions in this country and because of events beyond our control in other parts of the world, it becomes increasingly important to develop and apply the further measures which may be necessary from time to time to control the gold value of our own dollar at home.

Our dollar is now altogether too greatly influenced by the accidents of international trade, by the internal policies of other nations and by political disturbance in other continents. Therefore

168

the United States must take firmly in its own hands the control of the gold value of our dollar. This is necessary in order to prevent dollar disturbances from swinging us away from our ultimate goal, namely, the continued recovery of our commodity prices.

As a further effective means to this end, I am going to establish a government market for gold in the United States. Therefore, under the clearly defined authority of existing law, I am authorizing the Reconstruction Finance Corporation to buy gold newly mined in the United States at prices to be determined from time to time after consultation with the Secretary of the Treasury and the President. Whenever necessary to the end in view, we shall also buy or sell gold in the world market.

My aim in taking this step is to establish and maintain continuous control.

This is a policy and not an expedient.

It is not to be used merely to offset a temporary fall in prices. We are thus continuing to move towards a managed currency.

You will recall the dire predictions made last Spring by those who did not agree with our common policies of raising prices by direct means. What actually happened stood out in sharp contrast with those predictions. Government credit is high, prices have risen in part. Doubtless prophets of evil still exist in our midst. But government credit will be maintained and a sound currency will accompany a rise in the American commodity price level.

11. PRESIDENTIAL PROCLAMATION REVALUING GOLD, JANUARY 31, 1934

BY THE PRESIDENT OF THE UNITED STATES OF AMERICA

A PROCLAMATION

WHEREAS, by virtue of Section 1 of the Act of Congress approved March 14, 1900 (31 Stat. L.45), the present weight of the gold dollar is fixed at twenty-five and eight tenths grains of gold nine tenths fine; and

WHEREAS, by Section 43, Title III of the Act approved May 12, 1933 (Public No. 10, 73d Congress), as amended by Section 12 of the Gold Reserve Act of 1934, it is provided in part as follows:

"Whenever the President finds, upon investigation, that (1) the foreign commerce of the United States is adversely affected by reason of the depreciation in the value of the currency of any other government or governments in relation to the present standard value of gold, or (2) action under this section is necessary in order to regulate and maintain the parity of currency issues of the United States, or (3) an economic emergency requires an expansion of credit, or (4) an expansion of credit is necessary to secure by international agreement a stabilization at proper levels of the currencies of various governments, the President is authorized, in his discretion—

"(a) To direct the Secretary of the Treasury to enter into agreements with the several Federal Reserve banks and with the Federal Reserve Board whereby the Federal Reserve Board will, and it is hereby authorized to, notwithstanding any provisions of law or rules and regulations to the contrary, permit such reserve banks to agree that they will, (1) conduct, pursuant to existing law, throughout specified periods, open market operations in obligations of the United States Government or corporations in which the United States is the majority stockholder, and (2) purchase directly and hold in portfolio for an agreed period or periods of time Treasury bills or other obligations of the United States Government in an aggregate sum of $3,000,000,000 in addition to those they may then hold, unless prior to the termination of such period or periods the Secretary shall consent to their sale. No suspension of reserve requirements of the Federal Reserve banks, under the terms of section 11 (c) of the Federal Reserve Act, necessitated by reason of operations under this section, shall require the imposition of the graduated tax upon any deficiency in reserves as provided in said section 11 (c). Nor shall it require any automatic increase in the rates of interest or discount charged by any Federal Reserve bank, as otherwise specified in that section. The Federal Reserve Board, with the approval of the Secretary of the Treasury, may require the Federal Reserve banks to take such action as may be necessary, in the judgment of the Board and of the Secretary of the Treasury, to prevent undue credit expansion.

"(b) If the Secretary, when directed by the President, is unable to secure the assent of the several Federal Reserve banks and the Federal Reserve Board to the agreements authorized in this section, or if operations under the above provisions prove to be inadequate to meet the purposes of this section, or if for any other reason additional measures are required in the judgment of the President to meet such purposes, then the President is authorized—

$$* \quad * \quad * \quad * \quad *$$

"(2) By proclamation to fix the weight of the gold dollar in grains nine tenths fine and also to fix the weight of the silver dollar in grains nine tenths fine at a definite fixed ratio in relation to the gold dollar at such amounts as he finds necessary from his investigation to stabilize domestic prices or to protect the foreign commerce against the adverse effect of depreciated foreign currencies, and to provide for the unlimited coinage of such gold and silver at the ratio so fixed, or in case the Government of the United States enters into an agreement with any government or governments under the terms of which the ratio between the value of gold and other currency issued by the United States and by any such government or governments is established, the President may fix the weight of the gold dollar in accordance with the ratio so agreed upon, and such gold dollar, the weight of which is so fixed, shall be the standard unit of value, and all forms of money issued or coined by the United States shall be maintained at a parity with this standard and it shall be the duty of the Secretary of the Treasury to maintain such parity, but in no event shall the weight of the gold dollar be fixed so as to reduce its present weight by more than 50 per centum. Nor shall the weight of the gold dollar be fixed in any event at more than 60 per centum of its present weight. The powers of the President specified in this paragraph shall be deemed to be separate, distinct, and continuing powers, and may be exercised by him, from time to time, severally or together, whenever and as the expressed objects of this section in his judgment may require; except that such powers shall expire two years after the date of enactment of the Gold Reserve Act of 1934 unless the President shall sooner declare the existing emergency ended, but the President may extend such period for not more than one additional year after such date by proclamation recognizing the continuance of such emergency"; and

WHEREAS, I find, upon investigation, that the foreign commerce of the United States is adversely affected by reason of the depreciation in the value of the currencies of other governments in relation to the present standard value of gold, and that an economic emergency requires an expansion of credit; and

WHEREAS, in my judgment, measures additional to those provided by subsection (a) of said Section 43 are required to meet the purposes of such Section; and

WHEREAS, I find, from my investigation, that, in order to stabilize domestic prices and to protect the foreign commerce against the adverse effect of depreciated foreign currencies, it is necessary to fix the weight of the gold dollar at $15\frac{5}{21}$ grains nine tenths fine,

NOW, THEREFORE, be it known that I, FRANKLIN D. ROOSEVELT, President of the United States, by virtue of the authority vested in me by Section 43, Title III of said Act of May 12, 1933, as amended, and by virtue of all other authority vested in me, do hereby proclaim, order, direct, declare and fix the weight of the gold dollar to be $15\frac{5}{21}$ grains nine tenths fine, from and after the date and hour of this proclamation. The weight of the silver dollar is not altered or affected in any manner by reason of this proclamation.

This proclamation shall remain in force and effect until and unless repealed or modified by act of Congress or by subsequent proclamation; and notice is hereby given that I reserve the right by virtue of the authority vested in me to alter or modify this proclamation as the interest of the United States may seem to require.

IN WITNESS WHEREOF I have hereunto set my hand and have caused the seal of the United States to be affixed.

DONE in the City of Washington at 3:10 o'clock in the afternoon, Eastern Standard Time, this 31st day of January, in the year of our Lord one thousand nine hundred and thirty-four, and of the Independence of the United States the one hundred and fifty-eighth.

(Seal)

FRANKLIN D. ROOSEVELT

BY THE PRESIDENT:
CORDELL HULL
SECRETARY OF STATE

12. PRESIDENTIAL PROCLAMATION "NATIONALIZING" SILVER, AUGUST 9, 1934

BY THE PRESIDENT OF THE UNITED STATES OF AMERICA

A PROCLAMATION

WHEREAS, by Paragraph (2) of Section 43, Title III, of the Act of Congress, approved May 12, 1933 (Public No. 10), as amended by the Gold Reserve Act of 1934, the President is authorized "By proclamation to fix the weight of the gold dollar in grains nine tenths fine and also to fix the weight of the silver dollar in grains nine tenths fine at a definite fixed ratio in relation to the gold dollar at such amounts as he finds necessary from his investigation to stabilize domestic prices or to protect the foreign commerce against the adverse effect of depreciated foreign currencies, and to provide for the unlimited coinage of such gold and silver at the ratio so fixed, *** "; and "The President, in addition to the authority to provide for the unlimited coinage of silver at the ratio so fixed, under such terms and conditions as he may prescribe, is further authorized to cause to be issued and delivered to the tenderer of silver for coinage, silver certificates in lieu of the standard silver dollars to which the tenderer would be entitled and in an amount in dollars equal to the number of coined standard silver dollars that the tenderer of such silver for coinage would receive in standard silver dollars"; and "The President is further authorized to issue silver certificates in such denominations as he may prescribe against any silver bullion, silver, or standard silver dollars in the Treasury not then held for redemption of any outstanding silver certificates, and to coin standard silver dollars or subsidiary currency for the redemption of such silver certificates"; and

WHEREAS, the Silver Purchase Act of 1934, approved June 19, 1934, provides in Sections 2, 5, and 7, in part, as follows:

"SEC. 2. It is hereby declared to be the policy of the United States that the proportion of silver to gold in the monetary stocks of the United States should be increased, with the ultimate objective of having and maintaining, one fourth of the monetary value of such stocks in silver."

"SEC. 5. The Secretary of the Treasury is authorized and directed to issue silver certificates in such denominations as he may from time to time prescribe in a face amount not less than the cost of all

173

silver purchased under the authority of section 3, and such certificates shall be placed in actual circulation. There shall be maintained in the Treasury as security for all silver certificates heretofore or hereafter issued and at the time outstanding an amount of silver in bullion and standard silver dollars of a monetary value equal to the face amount of such silver certificates. All silver certificates heretofore or hereafter issued shall be legal tender for all debts, public and private, public charges, taxes, duties, and dues, and shall be redeemable on demand at the Treasury of the United States in standard silver dollars; and the Secretary of the Treasury is authorized to coin standard silver dollars for such redemption."

"SEC. 7. Whenever in the judgment of the President such action is necessary to effectuate the policy of this Act, he may by Executive order require the delivery to the United States mints of any or all silver by whomever owned or possessed. The silver so delivered shall be coined into standard silver dollars or otherwise added to the monetary stocks of the United States as the President may determine; and there shall be returned therefor in standard silver dollars, or any other coin or currency of the United States, the monetary value of the silver so delivered less such deductions for seigniorage, brassage, coinage, and other mint charges as the Secretary of the Treasury with the approval of the President shall have determined: *Provided,* That in no case shall the value of the amount returned therefor be less than the fair value at the time of such order of the silver required to be delivered as such value is determined by the market price over a reasonable period terminating at the time of such order. ****"

Now, THEREFORE, finding it necessary, in my judgment, to effectuate the policy of the Silver Purchase Act of 1934, to assist in increasing and stabilizing domestic prices, to protect our foreign commerce against the adverse effect of depreciated foreign currencies, and to promote the objectives of the Proclamation of the 21st day of December, nineteen hundred and thirty-three, relating to the coinage of silver; by virtue of the power in me vested by the Acts of Congress above cited, and other legislation designated for national recovery, and by virtue of all other authority in me vested;

I, FRANKLIN D. ROOSEVELT, PRESIDENT OF THE UNITED STATES OF AMERICA, do proclaim and direct that each United States mint shall receive for coinage or for addition to the monetary stocks of the United States, as hereinafter determined, any silver which such mint, subject to regulations prescribed hereunder by the Secretary of the Treasury, is satisfied was situated on the effective date hereof in the continental United States, including the Territory of Alaska.

The silver so delivered shall be added to the monetary stocks of the United States and shall be coined from time to time into standard silver dollars in such amounts as are required to carry out the provisions of this Proclamation and to provide for the redemption of silver certificates; and there shall be returned therefor in standard silver dollars, silver certificates, or any other coin or currency of the United States, the monetary value of the silver so delivered (that is, $1.2929+ a fine troy ounce), less a deduction of $61\frac{8}{25}$ percent thereof for seigniorage, brassage, coinage, and other mint charges, such deduction having been determined by the Secretary of the Treasury with my approval.

The provisions hereof are supplemental to the provisions of the Proclamation of the 21st day of December, nineteen hundred and thirty-three, and the United States coinage mints shall continue to receive for coinage in accordance with the provisions of such Proclamation silver which such mint, subject to regulations prescribed thereunder by the Secretary of the Treasury, is satisfied has been mined subsequently to the date of such Proclamation, from natural deposits in the United States or any place subject to the jurisdiction thereof; *provided, however,* that the Director of the Mint shall, at the option of the tenderer of such silver, deliver silver certificates in lieu of the standard silver dollars to which the tenderer of such silver for coinage would be entitled and in an amount in dollars equal to the coined standard silver dollars that the tenderer of such silver for coinage would receive in standard silver dollars.

The Secretary of the Treasury is authorized to prescribe regulations to carry out the purpose of this Proclamation.

Notice is hereby given that I reserve the right by virtue of the authority vested in me to revoke or modify this Proclamation as the interest of the United States may seem to require.

This Proclamation shall bear the date of, and becomes effective on, the day on which the Secretary or Acting Secretary of State countersigns the same, affixes thereto the Seal of the United States, and deposits this Proclamation so countersigned and sealed in the Office of the Secretary of State, as a part of the archives of the Nation.

IN WITNESS WHEREOF I have hereunto set my hand.

FRANKLIN D. ROOSEVELT

By the President; and countersigned and
sealed with the Seal of the United States,
by direction of the President, this 9th day
of August, in the year of our Lord nineteen
hundred and thirty-four, and of the Independence of
the United States of America the one hundred and fifty-ninth

CORDELL HULL
Secretary of State

13. GOLD STANDARD ACT, MARCH 14, 1900

AN ACT TO define and fix the standard of value, to maintain the parity of all forms of money issued or coined by the United States, to refund the public debt, and for other purposes.

Be it enacted by the Senate and House of Representatives of the United States of America in Congress assembled, That the dollar consisting of twenty-five and eight-tenths grains of gold nine-tenths fine, as established by section thirty-five hundred and eleven of the Revised Statutes of the United States, shall be the standard unit of value, and all forms of money issued or coined by the United States shall be maintained at a parity of value with this standard, and it shall be the duty of the Secretary of the Treasury to maintain such parity.

SEC. 2. That United States notes, and Treasury notes issued under the act of July fourteenth, eighteen hundred and ninety, when presented to the Treasury for redemption, shall be redeemed in gold coin of the standard fixed in the first section of this act, and in order to secure the prompt and certain redemption of such notes as herein provided it shall be the duty of the Secretary of the Treasury to set apart in the Treasury a reserve fund of one hundred and fifty million dollars in gold coin and bullion, which fund shall be used for such redemption purposes only, and whenever and as often as any of said notes shall be redeemed from said fund it shall be the duty of the Secretary of the Treasury to use said notes so redeemed to restore and maintain such reserve fund in the manner following, to wit: First, by exchanging the notes so redeemed for any gold coin in the general fund of the Treasury; second, by accepting deposits of gold coin at the Treasury or at any subtreasury in exchange for the United States notes so redeemed; third, by procuring gold coin by the use of said notes, in accordance with the provisions of section thirty-seven hundred of the Revised Statutes of the United States. If the Secretary of the Treasury is unable to restore and maintain the gold coin in the reserve fund by the foregoing methods, and the amount of such gold coin and bullion in said fund shall at any time fall below one hundred million dollars, then it shall be his duty to restore the same to the maximum sum of one hundred and fifty million dollars by borrowing money on the credit of the United States, and for the debt thus incurred to issue and sell coupon or registered bonds of the United States, in such form as he may prescribe, in denominations of fifty dollars or any multiple thereof, bearing interest at the rate of not exceeding three per centum per annum, payable quarterly, such bonds to be payable at the pleasure of the United States after one year from the date of their issue, and to be payable, principal and interest, in gold coin of the present standard value and to be exempt from the payment of all taxes or duties of the United States, as well as from taxation in any form by or under State, municipal, or local authority; and the gold coin received from the sale of said bonds shall first be covered into the general fund of the Treasury and then exchanged, in the manner hereinbefore provided, for an equal amount of the notes redeemed and held for exchange, and the Secretary of the Treasury may, in his discretion, use said notes in exchange for gold, or to purchase or redeem any bonds of the United States, or for any other lawful purpose the public interests may require, except that they shall not be used to meet deficiencies in the current revenues. That United States notes when redeemed in accordance with the provisions of this section shall be reissued, but shall be held in the reserve fund until exchanged for gold, as herein provided; and the gold coin and bullion in the reserve fund, together with the redeemed notes held for use as provided in this section, shall at no time exceed the maximum sum of one hundred and fifty million dollars.

SEC. 3. That nothing contained in this act shall be construed to affect the legal-tender quality as now provided by law of the silver dollar, or of any other money coined or issued by the United States.

SEC. 4. That there be established in the Treasury Department, as a part of the office of the Treasurer of the United States, divisions to be designated and known as the division of issue and the division of redemption, to which shall be assigned, respectively, under such regulations as the Secretary of the Treasury may approve, all records and accounts relating to the issue and redemption of United States notes, gold certificates, silver certificates, and currency certificates. There shall be transferred from the accounts of the general fund of the Treasury of the United States, and taken up on the books of said divisions, respectively, accounts relating to the reserve fund for the redemption of United States notes and Treasury notes, the gold coin held against outstanding gold certificates, the United States notes held against outstanding currency certificates, and the silver dollars held against outstanding silver certificates, and each of the funds represented by these accounts shall be used for the redemption of the notes and certificates for which they are respectively pledged, and shall be used for no other purpose, the same being held as trust funds.

SEC. 5. That it shall be the duty of the Secretary of the Treasury, as fast as standard silver dollars are coined under the provisions of the acts of July fourteenth, eighteen hundred and ninety, and June thirteenth, eighteen hundred and ninety-eight, from bullion purchased under the Act of July fourteenth, eighteen hundred and ninety, to retire and cancel an equal amount of Treasury notes whenever received into the Treasury, either by exchange in accordance with the provisions of this act or in the ordinary course of business, and upon the cancelation of Treasury notes silver certificates shall be issued against the silver dollars so coined.

SEC. 6. That the Secretary of the Treasury is hereby authorized and directed to receive deposits of gold coin with the Treasurer or any assistant treasurer of the United States in sums of not less than twenty dollars, and to issue gold certificates therefor in denominations of not less than twenty dollars, and the coin so deposited shall be retained in the Treasury and held for the payment of such certificates on demand, and used for no other purpose. Such certificates shall be receivable for customs, taxes, and all public dues, and when so received may be reissued, and when held by any national banking association may be counted as a part of its lawful reserve: *Provided,* That whenever and so long as the gold coin held in the reserve fund in the Treasury for the redemption of United States notes and Treasury notes shall fall and remain below one hundred million dollars the authority to issue certificates as herein provided shall be suspended: *And provided further,* That whenever and so long as the aggregate amount of United States notes and silver certificates in the general fund of the Treasury shall exceed sixty million dollars the Secretary of the Treasury may, in his discretion, suspend the issue of the certificates herein provided for: *And provided further,* That of the amount of such outstanding certificates one-fourth at least shall be in denominations of fifty dollars or less: *And provided further,* That the Secretary of the Treasury may, in his discretion, issue such certificates in denominations of ten thousand dollars, payable to order. And section fifty-one hundred and ninety-three of the Revised Statutes of the United States is hereby repealed.

SEC. 7. That hereafter silver certificates shall be issued only of denominations of ten dollars and under, except that not exceeding the aggregate ten per centum of the total volume of said certificates, in the discretion of the Secretary of the Treasury, may be issued in denominations of twenty dollars, fifty dollars, and one hundred dollars; and silver certificates of higher denomination than ten dollars, except as herein provided, shall, whenever received at the Treasury or redeemed, be retired and canceled, and certificates of denominations of ten dollars or less shall be substituted therefor, and after such substitution, in whole or in part, a like volume of

United States notes of less denomination than ten dollars shall from time to time be retired and canceled, and notes of denominations of ten dollars and upward shall be reissued in substitution therefor, with like qualities and restrictions as those retired and canceled.

SEC. 8. That the Secretary of the Treasury is hereby authorized to use, at his discretion, any silver bullion in the Treasury of the United States purchased under the Act of July fourteenth, eighteen hundred and ninety, for coinage into such denominations of subsidiary silver coin as may be necessary to meet the public requirements for such coin: *Provided,* That the amount of subsidiary silver coin outstanding shall not at any time exceed in the aggregate one hundred millions of dollars. Whenever any silver bullion purchased under the Act of July fourteenth, eighteen hundred and ninety, shall be used in the coinage of subsidiary silver coin, an amount of Treasury notes issued under said Act equal to the cost of the bullion contained in such coin shall be canceled and not reissued.

SEC. 9. That the Secretary of the Treasury is hereby authorized and directed to cause all worn and uncurrent subsidiary silver coin of the United States now in the Treasury, and hereafter received, to be recoined, and to reimburse the Treasurer of the United States for the difference between the nominal or face value of such coin and the amount the same will produce in new coin from any moneys in the Treasury not otherwise appropriated.

SEC. 10. That section fifty-one hundred and thirty-eight of the Revised Statutes is hereby amended so as to read as follows:

"Section 5138. No association shall be organized with a less capital than one hundred thousand dollars, except that banks with a capital of not less than fifty thousand dollars may, with the approval of the Secretary of the Treasury, be organized in any place the population of which does not exceed six thousand inhabitants, and except that banks with a capital of not less than twenty-five thousand dollars may, with the sanction of the Secretary of the Treasury, be organized in any place the population of which does not exceed three thousand inhabitants. No association shall be organized in a city the population of which exceeds fifty thousand persons with a capital of less than two hundred thousand dollars."

SEC. 11. That the Secretary of the Treasury is hereby authorized to receive at the Treasury any of the outstanding bonds of the United States bearing interest at five per centum per annum, payable February first, nineteen hundred and four, and any bonds of the United States bearing interest at four per centum per annum, payable July first, nineteen hundred and seven, and any bonds of the United States bearing interest at three per centum per annum, payable August first, nineteen hundred and eight, and to issue in exchange therefor an equal amount of coupon or registered bonds of the United States in such form as he may prescribe, in denominations of fifty dollars or any multiple thereof, bearing interest at the rate of two per centum per annum, payable quarterly, such bonds to be payable at the pleasure of the United States after thirty years from the date of their issue, and said bonds to be payable, principal and interest, in gold coin of the present standard value, and to be exempt from the payment of all taxes or duties of the United States, as well as from taxation in any form by or under State, municipal, or local authority: *Provided,* That such outstanding bonds may be received in exchange at a valuation not greater than their present worth to yield an income of two and one-quarter per centum per annum; and in consideration of the reduction of interest effected, the Secretary of the Treasury is authorized to pay to the holders of the outstanding bonds surrendered for exchange, out of any money in the Treasury not otherwise appropriated, a sum not greater than the difference between their present worth, computed as aforesaid, and their par value, and the payments to be made hereunder shall be held to be payments on account of the sinking fund created by section thirty-six hundred and ninety-four of the Revised Statutes: *And provided further,* That the two per centum bonds to be issued under the provisions of this Act shall be issued at not less than par, and they shall be numbered consecutively in the order of their issue, and when payment is made the last numbers issued shall be first paid, and this order shall be followed until all the bonds are paid, and whenever any of the outstanding bonds are called for payment interest thereon shall cease three months after such call; and there is hereby appropriated out of any money in the Treasury not otherwise appropriated, to effect the exchanges of bonds provided for in this Act, a sum not exceeding one-fifteenth of one per centum of the face value of said bonds, to pay the expense of preparing and issuing the same and other expenses incident thereto.

SEC. 12. That upon the deposit with the Treasurer of the United States, by any national banking association, of any bonds of the United States in the manner provided by existing law, such association shall be entitled to receive from the Comptroller of the Currency circulating notes in blank, registered and countersigned as provided by law, equal in amount to the par value of the bonds so deposited; and any national banking association now having bonds on deposit for the security of circulating notes, and upon which an amount of circulating notes has been issued less than the par value of the bonds, shall be entitled, upon due application to the Comptroller of the Currency, to receive additional circulating notes in blank to an amount which will increase the circulating notes held by such association to the par value of the bonds deposited, such additional notes to be held and treated in the same way as circulating notes of national banking associations heretofore issued, and subject to all the provisions of law affecting such notes: *Provided,* That nothing herein contained shall be construed to modify or repeal the provisions of section fifty-one hundred and sixty-seven of the Revised Statutes of the United States, authorizing the Comptroller of the Currency to require additional deposits of bonds or of lawful money in case the market value of the bonds held to secure the circulating notes shall fall below the par value of the circulating notes outstanding for which such bonds may be deposited as security: *And provided further,* That the circulating notes furnished to national banking associations under the provisions of this Act shall be of the denominations prescribed by law, except that no national banking association shall after the passage of this Act, be entitled to receive from the Comptroller of the Currency, or to issue or reissue or place in circulation, more than one-third in amount of its circulating notes of the denomination of five dollars: *And provided further,* That the total amount of such notes issued to any such association may equal at any time but shall not exceed the amount at such time of its capital stock actually paid in: *And provided further,* That under regulations to be prescribed by the Secretary of the Treasury any national banking association may substitute the two per centum bonds issued under the provisions of this Act for any of the bonds deposited with the Treasurer to secure circulation or to secure deposits of public money; and so much of an Act entitled "An Act to enable national banking associations to extend their corporate existence, and for other purposes," approved July twelfth, eighteen hundred and eighty-two, as prohibits any national bank which makes any deposit of lawful money in order to withdraw its circulating notes from receiving any increase of its circulation for the period of six months from the time it made such deposit of lawful money for the purpose aforesaid, is hereby repealed, and all other Acts or parts of Acts inconsistent with the provisions of this section are hereby repealed.

SEC. 13. That every national banking association having on deposit, as provided by law, bonds of the United States bearing interest at the rate of two per centum per annum, issued under the provisions of this act, to secure its circulating notes, shall pay to the Treasury of the United States, in the months of January and July, a tax of one-fourth of one per centum each half year upon the average amount of such of its notes in circulation as are based upon the deposit of said two per centum bonds; and such taxes shall be in lieu of existing taxes on its notes in circulation imposed by section fifty-two hundred and fourteen of the Revised Statutes.

SEC. 14. That the provisions of this Act are not intended to preclude the accomplishment of international bimetallism whenever conditions shall make it expedient and practicable to secure the same by concurrent action of the leading commercial nations of the world and at a ratio which shall insure permanence of relative value between gold and silver.

Approved, March 14, 1900

14. PRESIDENT'S GOLD MESSAGE, JANUARY 15, 1934

MESSAGE

FROM

THE PRESIDENT OF THE UNITED STATES

REQUESTING

CERTAIN ADDITIONAL LEGISLATION TO IMPROVE THE FINANCIAL AND MONETARY SYSTEM OF THE UNITED STATES

To the Congress:

In conformity with the progress we are making in restoring a fairer price level and with our purpose of arriving eventually at a less variable purchasing power for the dollar, I ask the Congress for certain additional legislation to improve our financial and monetary system. By making clear that we are establishing permanent metallic reserves in the possession and ownership of the Federal Government, we can organize a currency system which will be both sound and adequate.

The issuance and control of the medium of exchange which we call "money" is a high prerogative of government. It has been such for many centuries. Because they were scarce, because they could readily be subdivided and transported, gold and silver have been used either for money or as a basis for forms of money which in themselves had only nominal intrinsic value.

In pure theory, of course, a government could issue mere tokens to serve as money—tokens which would be accepted at their face value if it were certain that the amount of these tokens were permanently limited and confined to the total amount necessary for the daily cash needs of the community. Because this assurance could not always or sufficiently be given, governments have found that reserves or bases of gold and silver behind their paper or token currency added stability to their financial systems.

There is still much confusion of thought which prevents a worldwide agreement creating a uniform monetary policy. Many advocate gold as the sole basis of currency; others advocate silver; still others advocate both gold and silver whether as separate bases, or on a basis with a fixed ratio, or on a fused basis.

We hope that, despite present world confusion, events are leading to some future form of general agreement. The recent London agreement in regard to silver was a step, though only a step, in this direction.

At this time we can usefully take a further step, which we hope will contribute to an ultimate world-wide solution.

Certain lessons seem clear. For example, the free circulation of gold coins is unnecessary, leads to hoarding, and tends to a possible weakening of national financial structures in times of emergency. The practice of transferring gold from one individual to another or from the Government to an individual within a nation is not only unnecessary but is in every way undesirable. The transfer of gold in bulk is essential only for the payment of international trade balances.

Therefore it is a prudent step to vest in the government of a nation the title to and possession of all monetary gold within its boundaries and to keep that gold in the form of bullion rather than in coin.

Because the safe-keeping of this monetary basis rests with the Government, we have already called in the gold which was in the possession of private individuals or corporations. There remains, however, a very large weight in gold bullion and coins which is still in the possession or control of the Federal Reserve banks.

Although under existing law there is authority, by Executive act, to take title to the gold in the possession or control of the Reserve banks, this is a step of such importance that I prefer to ask the Congress by specific enactment to vest in the United States Government title to all supplies of American-owned monetary gold, with provision for the payment therefor in gold certificates. These gold certificates will be, as now, secured at all times dollar for dollar by gold in the Treasury—gold for each dollar of such weight and fineness as may be established from time to time.

Such legislation places the right, title, and ownership to our gold reserves in the Government itself; it makes clear the Government's ownership of any added dollar value of the country's stock of gold which would result from any decrease of the gold content of the dollar which may be made in the public interest. It would also, of course, with equal justice, cast upon the Government the loss of such dollar value if the public interest in the future should require an increase in the amount of gold designated as a dollar.

The title to all gold being in the Government, the total stock will serve as a permanent and fixed metallic reserve which will change in amount only so far as necessary for the settlement of international balances or as may be required by a future agreement among the nations of the world for a redistribution of the world stock of monetary gold.

With the establishment of this permanent policy, placing all monetary gold in the ownership of the Government as a bullion base for its currency, the time has come for a more certain determination of the gold value of the American dollar. Because of world uncertainties, I do not believe it desirable in the public interest that an exact value be now fixed. The President is authorized by present legislation to fix the lower limit of permissible revaluation at 50 percent. Careful study leads me to believe that any revaluation at more than 60 percent of the present statutory value would not be in the public interest. I, therefore, recommend to the Congress that it fix the upper limit of permissible revaluation at 60 percent.

That we may be further prepared to bring some greater degree of stability to foreign exchange rates in the interests of our people, there should be added to the present power of the Secretary of the Treasury to buy and sell gold at home and abroad, express power to deal in foreign exchange as such. As a part of this power, I suggest that, out of the profits of any devaluation, there should be set up a fund of $2,000,000,000 for such purchases and sales of gold, foreign exchange, and Government securities as the regulation of the currency, the maintenance of the credit of the Government, and the general welfare of the United States may require.

Certain amendments of existing legislation relating to the purchase and sale of gold and to other monetary matters would add to the convenience of handling current problems in this field. The Secretary of the Treasury is prepared to submit information concerning such changes to the appropriate committees of the Congress.

The foregoing recommendations relate chiefly to gold. The other principal precious metal—silver—has also been used from time immemorial as a metallic base for currencies as well as for actual currency itself. It is used as such by probably half the population of the world. It constitutes a very important part of our own monetary structure. It is such a crucial factor in much of the world's international trade that it cannot be neglected.

On December 21, 1933, I issued a proclamation providing for the coinage of our newly mined silver and for increasing our reserves of silver bullion, thereby putting us among the first nations to carry out the silver agreement entered into by 66 governments at the London Conference. This agreement is distinctly a step in the right direction and we are proceeding to perform our part of it.

All of the 66 nations agreed to refrain from melting or debasing their silver coins, to replace paper currency of small denominations with silver coins, and to refrain from legislation that would depreciate the value of silver in the world markets. Those nations producing large quantities of silver agreed to take specified amounts from their domestic production and those holding and using large quantities agreed to restrict the amount they would sell during the 4 years covered by the agreement.

If all these undertakings are carried out by the governments concerned, there will be a marked increase in the use and value of silver.

Governments can well, as they have in the past, employ silver as a basis for currency, and I look for a greatly increased use. I am, however, withholding any recommendation to the Congress looking to further extension of the monetary use of silver because I believe that we should gain more knowledge of the results of the London agreement and of our other monetary measures.

Permit me once more to stress two principles. Our national currency must be maintained as a sound currency which, insofar as possible, will have a fairly constant standard of purchasing power and be adequate for the purposes of daily use and the establishment of credit.

The other principle is the inherent right of government to issue currency and to be the sole custodian and owner of the base or reserve of precious metals underlying that currency. With this goes the prerogative of government to determine from time to time the extent and nature of the metallic reserve. I am confident that the Nation will well realize the definite purpose of the Government to maintain the credit of that Government and, at the same time, to provide a sound medium of exchange which will serve the needs of our people.

FRANKLIN D. ROOSEVELT

THE WHITE HOUSE
January 15, 1934

15. PRESIDENT'S SILVER MESSAGE, MAY 22, 1934

To the Congress of the United States:

On January 11, 1934,[1] I recommended to the Congress legislation which was promptly exacted under the title, "The Gold Reserve Act of 1934." This Act vested in the United States Government the custody and control of our stocks of gold as a reserve for our paper currency and as a medium of settling international balances. It set up a stabilization fund for the control of foreign exchange in the interests of our people, and certain amendments were added to facilitate the acquisition of silver.

As stated in my message to the Congress, this legislation was recommended as a step in improving our financial and monetary system. Its enactment has laid a foundation on which we are organizing a currency system that will be both sound and adequate. It is a long step forward, but only a step.

As a part of the larger objective, some things have been clear. One is that we should move forward as rapidly as conditions permit in broadening the metallic base of our monetary system and in stabilizing the purchasing and debt paying power of our money on a more equitable level. Another is that we should not neglect the value of an increased use of silver in improving our monetary system. Since 1929 that has been obvious.

Some measures for making a greater use of silver in the public interest are appropriate for independent action by us. On others, international cooperation should be sought.

Of the former class is that of increasing the proportion of silver in the abundant metallic reserves back of our paper currency. This policy was initiated by the Proclamation of December 21, 1933, bringing our current domestic production of silver into the Treasury, as well as placing this nation among the first to carry out the agreement on silver which we sought and secured at the London Conference. We have since acquired other silver in the interest of stabilization of foreign exchange and the development of a broader metallic base for our currency. We seek to remedy a maladjustment of our currency.

In further aid of this policy, it would be helpful to have legislation broadening the authority for the further acquisition and monetary use of silver.

I, therefore, recommend legislation at the present session declaring it to be the policy of the United States to increase the amount of silver in our monetary stocks with the ultimate objective of hav-

[1] January 15?

ing and maintaining one-fourth of their monetary value in silver
and three-fourths in gold.

The Executive Authority should be authorized and directed to
make the purchases of silver necessary to attain this ultimate
objective.

The authority to purchase present accumulations of silver in
this country should be limited to purchases at not in excess of
50 cents per ounce.

The Executive Authority should be enabled, should circumstances require, to take over present surpluses of silver in this
country not required for industrial uses on payment of just compensation, and to regulate imports, exports and other dealings in
monetary silver.

There should be a tax of at least 50 percent on the profits accruing from dealing in silver.

We can proceed with this program of increasing our store of
silver for use as a part of the metallic reserves for our paper currency without seriously disturbing adjustments in world trade.
However, because of the great world supply of silver and its use
in varying forms by the world's population, concerted action by
all nations, or at least a large group of nations, is necessary if a
permanent measure of value, including both gold and silver, is
eventually to be made a world standard. To arrive at that point, we
must seek every possibility for world agreement, although it may turn
out that this nation will ultimately have to take such independent
action on this phase of the matter as its interests require.

The success of the London Conference in consummating an international agreement on silver, which has now been ratified by all
the governments concerned, makes such further agreement worth
seeking. The ebb and flow of values in almost all parts of the world
have created many points of pressure for readjustments of internal
and international standards. At no time since the efforts of this
nation to secure international agreement on silver began in 1878
have conditions been more favorable for making progress along
this line.

Accordingly, I have begun to confer with some of our neighbors
in regard to the use of both silver and gold, preferably on a co-
ordinated basis, as a standard of monetary value. Such an agreement would constitute an important step forward toward a
monetary unit of value more equitable and stable in its purchasing
and debt paying power.

FRANKLIN D. ROOSEVELT

THE WHITE HOUSE
  May 22, 1934

BIBLIOGRAPHY

Academy of Political Science. *Proceedings.*
Vol. XV.   No. 1   *The Crisis in World Finance and Trade* (May, 1932).
No. 3 *Tariffs and Trade Barriers* (June, 1933).
Vol. XVI.   No. 1 *Money and Credit in the Recovery Program* (April, 1934).
Vol. XVII. No. 1 *Economic Recovery and Monetary Stabilization* (May, 1936).

Angell, J. W., "Exchange Depreciation, Foreign Trade and National Welfare." *Proceedings* of the Academy of Political Science. XV (1933), No. 3, 9-20.

——— "The Federal Finances and the Banking System." *Journal of the American Statistical Association.* XXX (1935), 169-174.

——— "Gold, Banks and the New Deal." *Political Science Quarterly.* XLIX (1934), 481-505.

Annalist, The (Weekly).

Barron's, the National Financial Weekly.

Berridge, W. A., "Some Facts Bearing on the Silver Program." *Review of Economic Statistics.* XVI (1934), 231-36.

Bratter, H. M., "The Currency of the United States." *Banking.* XXVIII (1935), 95-104.

Carothers, N., *Silver in America.* Bulletin No. 11 prepared for the Commission on Banking Law and Practice, Association of Reserve City Bankers. Chicago, July, 1936.

Chase Economic Bulletin (Written by Dr. B. M. Anderson, Jr., Economist of the Chase National Bank of the City of New York).

Commercial and Financial Chronicle (Weekly).

Commission of Inquiry into National Policy in International Economic Relations, *Report.* Minneapolis. University of Minnesota Press, 1934.

Federal Reserve Bank of New York, *Annual Report.*

——— *Monthly Review.*

Federal Reserve System, Board of Governors of (formerly the Federal Reserve Board), *Annual Report.*

——— *The Federal Reserve Act, as Amended.* Compiled under the direction of the Board, in the Office of its General Counsel.

——— *Federal Reserve Bulletin* (Monthly).

——— *Weekly Review of Periodicals* (Mimeographed).

Gayer, A. D., *Monetary Policy and Economic Stabilization.* New York, 1935.

Handy and Harman, *Annual Review of the Silver Market*. New York.

Hutchins, R. M., "The Future of World Trade." *Economic Forum*. III (summer, 1935), 133–48.

Kemmerer, E. W., *Kemmerer on Money*. 2d ed. Philadelphia, 1934.

Leavens, D. H., "American Silver Policy and China." *Harvard Business Review*. XIV (1935–36), 45–58.

—— "The Distribution of the World's Silver." *Review of Economic Statistics*. XVII (1935), 131–38.

—— "Silver and the Business Depression." *Harvard Business Review*. IX (1930–31), 330–38.

—— "Silver Coins to the Melting Pot." *Annalist*. XLVI (1935), 3–5.

Lloyd's Bank Limited (London), *Monthly Review*.

Manufacturers Trust Company, New York, *The Gold Clause Cases*. A reprint of the full text of the opinions of the Supreme Court of the United States, a brief analysis of the decisions, and a summary of the points of counsel. 1935.

National City Bank of New York, *Monthly Letter on Economic Conditions*.

National Industrial Conference Board, *The New Monetary System of the United States* (Prepared by Professor R. A. Young). New York, 1934.

New York *Times* (Daily).

New York Trust Company, *The Index* (Monthly through 1937; now Quarterly).

Pasvolsky, Leo, *Current Monetary Issues*. Washington, 1933.

Pittman, Key, "Silver in Our Monetary System." *Proceedings* of the Academy of Political Science. XVI (1934), No. 1, 27–36.

Reconstruction Finance Corporation, *Public Advertisement Regarding Notes of the Reconstruction Finance Corporation, Series of February 1, 1934*. Circular No. 12. October 26, 1933.

—— *Quarterly Reports*.

Sprague, O. M. W., *Recovery and Common Sense*. Boston and New York, 1934.

United States Congress, House of Representatives

Committee on Appropriations, Subcommittee for the Treasury and Post Office Departments, *Treasury Department Appropriation Bill for 1938; Hearings*. 75th Congress, 1st Session. 1937.

Committee on Banking and Currency, *Gold Clause Securities; Hearings on H. J. Res. 348 (H.J.Res. 339)*. 74th Congress, 1st Session. 1935.

—— *Liberalizing the Credit Facilities of the Federal Reserve System; Hearings on H. R. 9203*. 72nd Congress, 1st Session. 1932.

Committee on Coinage, Weights and Measures, *Gold Reserve Act of 1934; Hearings on H. R. 6976*. 73rd Congress, 2d Session. 1934.

Committee on the Revision of the Laws, *The Code of the Laws of the United States of America*.

Committee on Ways and Means, *Silver Purchase Act of 1934; Hearings on H. R. 9745*. 73rd Congress, 2d Session. 1934.

United States Congress, National Monetary Commission, *Laws of the United States Concerning Money, Banking and Loans, 1778–1909*. 61st Congress, 2nd Session, Senate Document No. 580. 1910.

United States Congress, Senate

Committee on Agriculture and Forestry, *Monetary Authority Act; Hearings on S. 1990*. 75th Congress, 1st Session. 1937.

Committee on Banking and Currency, *Gold Reserve Act of 1934; Hearings on S. 2366*. 73rd Congress, 2d Session. 1934.

———— *Gold-Clause Securities of the United States; Hearings on S. J. Res. 155*. 74th Congress, 1st Session. 1935.

United States Department of Commerce, Bureau of Foreign and Domestic Commerce, *Handbook of Foreign Currencies*. Trade Promotion Series No. 164. 1936 (Revision of Trade promotion Series No. 102, published in 1930).

———— *The Monetary Use of Silver in 1933*. By H. M. Bratter. Trade Promotion Series No. 149. 1933.

———— *Survey of Current Business* (Monthly).

———— *World Economic Review* (Annually; first issued as of 1933).

United States Department of State, *Executive Agreement Series* (International agreements, other than treaties, to which the United States is a party).

———— *Press Releases* (Weekly printed edition of daily mimeographed press releases of the Department).

———— *Session Laws* (Issued at the close of each Congressional Session).

———— *Statutes at Large* (Issued at the close of each Congress).

———— *Treaty Information* (Monthly Bulletin).

United States President

Important Proclamations

March 6, 1933. Proclaiming the bank holiday.

March 9, 1933. Continuing the bank holiday.

December 21, 1933. Providing for the purchase of newly mined domestic silver.

January 31, 1934. Reducing the weight of the gold dollar.

August 9, 1934. "Nationalizing" silver.

April 10, 1935. Raising price of newly mined domestic silver.

April 24, 1935. Raising, again, price of newly mined domestic silver.

December 31, 1937. Reducing price of newly mined domestic silver.

Messages to Congress

January 15, 1934. Concerning the Gold Reserve Act of 1934.

May 22, 1934. Concerning the Silver Purchase Act of 1934.

Radio Address of the President. Delivered from the White House, October 22, 1933.

United States Superintendent of Documents, *Congressional Record,* 1933–37, *passim.*

United States Supreme Court, *Gold Clauses in Obligations.* Opinions of the Supreme Court of the United States and the Dissenting Opinions, in the cases questioning the validity of the Joint Resolution of Congress of June 5, 1933, with respect to the "Gold Clauses" in obligations. 74th Congress, 1st Session, Senate Document No. 21. 1935 (Decisions also reprinted by Manufacturers Trust Company, New York, *q.v. supra*).

United States Treasury Department

Bureau of the Mint, *Annual Report of the Director of the Mint.*

——— *Monetary Units and Coinage Systems of the Principal Countries of the World.* 1929.

Comptroller of the Currency, *Annual Report.*

Office of the Secretary, *Annual Report of the Secretary of the Treasury on the State of the Finances.*

——— *Daily Statement of the United States Treasury.*

——— *Documents and Statements Pertaining to the Banking Emergency.* 1933.

——— *Gold regulations,* issued under various Acts, executive orders, etc.

——— Miscellaneous press releases.

——— Miscellaneous proclamations, orders and regulations.

——— *Silver regulations,* issued under various Acts, executive orders, etc.

——— *Statement of the Public Debt* (Issued Monthly).

Public Debt Service, *Circulation Statement of United States Money* (Issued Monthly).

Treasurer of the United States, *Annual Report.*

INDEX

INDEX